HOW TO TURN $100 INTO $1,000,000

by James McKenna and Jeannine Glista
with Matt Fontaine

Workman Publishing
New York

We would like to thank the following people and organizations who helped make this book possible: America's Credit Unions, for generously funding the *Biz Kid$* TV series and financial literacy outreach initiatives. Steve Birge, for additional writing, and Pam Whalley from the Council for Economic Education and George Burdick from Merrill Lynch, for content review (and for checking our math!). Last, but not least, we are grateful to the entire team at Workman and our editor extraordinaire, Justin Krasner, for patiently guiding this project with wit, wisdom, and humor.

Library of Congress Cataloging-in-Publication Data is available.

ISBN 978-0-7611-8080-7

Design by Colleen AF Venable

Illustrations by Emma Cook

Workman books are available at special discounts when purchased in bulk for premiums and sales promotions as well as for fund-raising or educational use. Special editions or book excerpts can also be created to specification. For details, contact the Special Sales Director at the address below or send an email to specialmarkets@workman.com.

Workman Publishing Co., Inc.
225 Varick Street
New York, NY 10014-4381
workman.com

WORKMAN is a registered trademark of Workman Publishing Co., Inc.

Printed in China

First printing March 2016

10 9

This book is for general information and educational purposes only and is not intended to be your only source of financial advice.

Contents

DISCLAIMER: This book is for information only. We can't be responsible for any profits or losses you might experience as a result of following the advice in this book. You could go out and invest in magic unicorn dust and then blame us. Uh-uh. Not gonna happen. Life is full of risk. Especially when it comes to money. Be smart; save, earn, and invest wisely; don't do dumb stuff; and you will have a much better chance of making a million dollars.

Introduction:
WHY $1,000,000?

$1 MILLION dollars. That's a one with six zeros behind it. Eight if you count pennies: $1,000,000.00. Yet today everybody talks about a billion dollars. That's a one with nine zeros behind it. Add two more for the pennies.

$1 million can be a lot of money . . . or not a lot of money. It's all relative. To most of us, $1 million is a lot of money.

If you stacked up a million one-dollar bills, it would be 350 feet tall! (That's around 107 meters for you readers in most of the world.) However, $1 million to a multimillionaire, or especially a billionaire? *Pffft.* Relatively speaking, that's chump change. It all comes down to perspective, and from where we sit, $1 million is still a lot of money.

OK, time to get serious. Not too serious. More like medium-serious with a side of clown shoes.

Not all of you who read this book will succeed at getting $1 million in your lifetime. In fact, most people will never reach that goal. If it were that easy, don't you think everybody would be a millionaire? I mean, c'mon.

Saving up $1 million is going to take commitment, hard work, and a little sacrifice. Anyone can do it, but most people don't. And in the long run, isn't that a small price to pay for your financial independence?

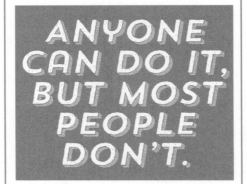

ANYONE CAN DO IT, BUT MOST PEOPLE DON'T.

Believe it or not, some people would say no. In fact, most people say no with their actions, even if they like the idea. Many not only fail to save today's money, but they also spend tomorrow's money with credit cards and **loans** they might not need. It's so easy for people to fall into the trap of trying to live beyond their means. They "live for today," but save nothing for tomorrow. And believe us, you'll want money for tomorrow.

HAVING MONEY IS GOOD. WHY?

1. FREEDOM. Money buys freedom. Period. If you have money, you have more choices. Don't like your boss? Quit your job. Don't like the neighborhood? Move to another one. Want to travel the world? Go ahead. Study ballet? Get out your tutu and pointe shoes because you can. That's the power of money.

2. SAFETY NET. Life is like a friendly-looking badger with a bad temper. One moment it's all smiles and affection, the next it's biting you on the arm. Having money and an **emergency fund** are protection against the angry badgers of life. Imagine that leg bite ended up costing you $100,000 in hospital bills. If you had $1 million, you could cover the cost and still have $900,000 left!

3. HELPING OTHERS. There is an old expression, "A rising tide floats all boats." You, your family, and your community can all benefit from you having money. Many millionaires, billionaires, and even thousandaires use some of their money to help not only themselves, but also others. They might create scholarships to send kids to college, donate to the arts, help the homeless, or even invest in a business. And yes, they still have money left over for their old age.

BUT WHY $1,000,000?

WE'RE not talking about greed here. We're talking about making money to support yourself. We're talking about **financial freedom,** versus financial servitude. A life filled with options, versus a life of **debt**. Maybe you don't think you need $1 million now, but eventually you'll need some money, unless you plan on living in your parents' basement your whole life. Even then, you'll still need money.

And that's where this book comes in. We've researched and interviewed hundreds of kids over the years to learn what they've done to go from nothing to making $1 million at a very early age. Through these observations, we hope to help you become one of those success stories as well.

By the way, when it comes to money, your past does not determine your future. No matter what your lot in life, no matter where you live or how you live—single parent, no parents, foster child, rich, poor, urban, rural, there are plenty of examples of people who have come from nothing to become something. And today it is easier to get to $1 million than at any other time in

Badgers are not your friends.

the history of the world. Of course, that's if you play your cards right and learn a few simple strategies like the ones we're going to share with you in this book.

And one of the first things you'll learn? The earlier you start earning and saving, the more time you'll have to grow your money.

Spoiler Alert: Luckily, you don't actu-ally have to save up the entire $1 million all by yourself. There's a little secret that we let you in on later in the book, where you just have to save up enough so that your money starts *making money for you*. We know! Kooky notion! But totally doable. Especially if you are young! That's why you need to make the deci-sion to start right now!

Downtown before the candy store opened up…

SWEET SUCCESS

We know a 15-year-old girl who opened a candy store in an abandoned building at the main intersection of a run-down area of town.

DREAM BIG

WHAT would you do with $1 million? Would you shred a gold-plated skateboard through the streets of Beverly Hills? Buy a plane and fly to a tropical island for lunch? Host fabulous parties at your massive penthouse apartment? Or, maybe your goals are a little more practical; you want money to go to college, buy a house one day, or help people in need. That's all possible if you have $1 million. So, what are you waiting for? Go save up $1 million! And make sure you have fun doing it!

...and downtown after!

Her business was a success, and new businesses soon moved into buildings on either side of her. Soon the downtown started coming back to life, all anchored by her thriving candy business.

Chapter 1:
THINK LIKE A MILLIONAIRE

WHAT do real millionaires look like? Are they tall, dark, and handsome? Some. Do they jet around the world, getting daily mani-pedis? Some. Do they drive a used car, live below their means, and stay under the radar? Most. Real millionaires come in all shapes and sizes. Sure, some of them may be hip, young movie stars, or **Wall Street** brokers, but not many. The simple truth is that millionaires are people who save money, not people who spend it.

Sure, that's not as dramatic as the

TV version of a millionaire, but it's also awesome because it means that almost anyone can become one. Even you. Even if you've never saved a dollar in your life. Even if you think you are not smart enough to try. You are, and you can do it.

HOW?

THERE actually is something you can start doing right now, and it's as easy as putting on a pair of flip-flops: Begin working on your Million-Dollar Mind-Set (MDM).

Having a Million-Dollar Mind-Set, more than anything, is all about attitude. It means you commit to a financial goal of making a million bucks. We're not talking about a half-baked commitment. We mean you really, truly commit. Like Dorothy-commited-to-finding-the-Emerald-City-so-she-could-get-back-home-to-Kansas kind of commitment. You decide that you can do this and that you are *worthy* of this. Because you are. Thinking like a millionaire means you commit to a goal and work to achieve the objective. You have to put yourself in the proper mind-set.

IGNORE THE BLING* AND DO YOUR OWN THING

RIGHT. Like all one has to do is *think* like a millionaire and *poof*, it happens. If it's so simple, why isn't everyone a millionaire? Because sticking to a financial plan over time can be pretty challenging. Everywhere you turn there's something to spend your money on, making it seem like as soon as you do you'll be happy, healthy, rich, popular, successful—whatever. It's hard to resist temptation, especially when it seems like everyone else is buying the latest phone or game or gadget.

THE MILLION-DOLLAR MIND-SET

One big secret to becoming a millionaire is *not* buying the latest thing just because everyone else has. Thinking like a millionaire means you find ways to save money instead of constantly spending it. Sometimes that means wearing last year's sneakers for one more year. Sometimes it means taking an extra shift at your job instead of going out with friends. It might even mean cooking ramen noodles instead of always going out for dinner.

* *"Bling" = any unnecessary accumulation of metal or jewelry that impresses the simpleminded.*

WAIT... THERE'S MORE!

SAVING more and spending less is definitely part of the MDM, but there's a little more to it than that. Having an MDM means you also have the following:

1. FOCUS.

Saving up $1 million is a very ambitious goal. To get there you have to stay focused. You may experience setbacks along the way—jobs that don't work out, investments that lose money, and most of all, so many tempting ways to spend money rather than save it. You must focus on ways to always be moving forward toward that ultimate destination.

2. PATIENCE.

We know, you want to be rich yesterday. Sure, some millionaires got that way in a flash—by winning the lottery, inheriting some money, or inventing a cool app, but that's a very small minority. Most millionaires built their savings over a period of time. They saved, invested, and waited, protecting their nest egg (aka "investments"), while continuing to add money on a regular basis and watching it grow over time.

KNOW YOUR NEIGHBORS

Back in 1996, a researcher named Thomas Stanley decided to look into what millionaires are really like. The book he wrote is called *The Millionaire Next Door*. What he found surprised many. Most wealthy people don't drive flashy cars or take expensive vacations. Quite the opposite. They spend much less than they earn, drive used cars, and live in modest houses. They invest their money wisely—and they don't buy things to make themselves look cool. Like we said—*actual millionaires are people who save money, not people who spend it.*

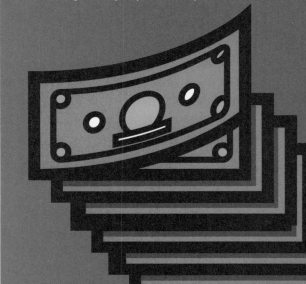

3. CONFIDENCE.

If you do what everybody else does, you'll be just like them, and *not* a millionaire. To save up all that cash, you'll need an independent mind-set. Don't be a sheep by following the crowd. Trying to impress people with the latest fashion, cars, or technology is the fastest way to not become a millionaire.

SAVE MORE, SPEND LESS.

4. KNOWLEDGE.

To become a millionaire, you'll need to understand money—how to save it, how to grow it, and how to keep it. Luckily, you can get that knowledge from this book!

MAKE MDM A HABIT

THANKS to generations of nail-biters and nose-pickers, the word *habit* has gotten a bad rap. You can, however, have good habits, and one of them would be to put away some money for yourself on a regular basis. That is one habit that almost every millionaire shares. They know how to make a mountain of money and they do it slowly, steadily, and on a regular basis.

Maybe the habit is as simple as saving a dollar a day. Too much? No worries. How about half that? Any amount is better than no amount. Developing good money habits takes time, but as with anything else, you start with the first step and work your way up.

DON'T GIVE UP!

EVEN the smartest millionaires can be hit with financial misfortune the likes of what occurred during the **Great Depression of the 1930s** and the **Great Recession of 2008**. Many people trying to advance their financial futures were hit hard during those two great economic downturns. Some were able to recover. Part of that is luck. Part is perseverance.

Michael Jordan, one of the most successful basketball players of all time, said, "I can accept failure; everyone fails at something. But I can't accept not trying." Even Thomas Edison failed at least 1,000 times trying to get the light-bulb right, but he eventually did, and changed history. Millionaires don't like failing, but many of them fail anyway. They know it's just part of the game.

They also know that if it happens, they learn from it and try again.

Don't be afraid to fail. Persevere through mistakes and struggles. Stay focused, patient, confident, and smart and you'll have a better chance of making money.

YOUR MILLION-DOLLAR PLAN

MOST millionaires and billionaires wouldn't have achieved their big financial goals if they didn't have a plan. In this book we will hold your hand (don't worry, not literally) through every step of creating your *own* plan to becoming financially independent (aka "rich"). We will teach you tips and tricks to becoming a millionaire, and point out the pitfalls along the way.

Making money is a game, and we're going to teach you the basic rules. Before we move on we want to make sure you are willing to commit. Can you think like a millionaire thinks? Can you be focused on the goal? Because if you can get into the Million-Dollar Mind-Set, and focus on earning and saving $1 million, you have a chance at making it. Start by looking at yourself confidently in the mirror and repeating the very important phrase on the next page. Go ahead, turn the page!

Thomas "Sparky" Edison

Michael "Air" Jordan

"I WILL BECOME A MILLIONAIRE."

LONG STORY SHORT

· ·

1. Millionaires are folks who save their money, not spend it.

2. To become a millionaire you need to develop an MDM (Million-Dollar Mind-Set).

3. Anyone can become a millionaire if you follow the above.

REASONS TO BECOME A MILLIONAIRE

What are some reasons why you want to turn $100 into $1 million? Write your reasons down, post them in your locker, stick them to the mirror, tape them to the ceiling above your bed, make them the background on your phone—just put them someplace where you can see them for daily inspiration. Your reasons will help keep you going through thick and thin. Don't think about it too hard—for now, just imagine what you'd do with that money. Your reasons will probably change over time, so keep the original list to remember when you started your journey to financial independence.

_____

_____

_____

_____

_____

_____

_____

_____

_____

_____

_____

Chapter 2:
SET FINANCIAL GOALS

FUTURE BANK

DATE 01/04/2035

10 000000 —

PAY TO THE ORDER OF ___ Me

Ten Million Dollars —

Me

FOR ___ Future Earnings

CHECKBOOK

WHAT kind of life do you want to live? Do you want to travel, help the poor, race dirt bikes, be a tech **mogul**, design dresses, navigate space, become a pro skateboarder, all of the above?

You'll have a better chance of achieving the life you want if you have money. And that means you'll need a plan, with financial goals.

A plan with financial goals will keep you from being adrift in an ocean of money. It's like charting a course for the "Island of Financial Freedom."

MONEY MOMENT

One way to help you with financial goals is to have separate accounts for different goals. You could have a **savings account** for your short-term goal of purchasing a new computer, put money into a **certificate of deposit (CD)** account for a medium-term goal of saving for college, and then invest in an **IRA** for your long-term goal of retirement. We know, we're getting a little ahead of ourselves when we talk about **investing** in a CD or an IRA. Guess you'll have to keep reading to figure out what that means! We'll talk more about different types of investments in chapter 9.

Without a plan and goals, you might end up on the rocks and never have enough money, particularly when you need it most.

Goal setting is not a one-time event. Some people have hourly, daily, weekly, monthly, quarterly, semi-yearly, yearly, 5-year, 10-year, 20-year, and even lifetime goals. For now, let's think about setting these three goals: **short-, medium-, and long-term goals**.

SHORT-TERM GOALS
(FROM NOW TO 1 YEAR)

Maybe you have a goal of saving enough money to go to that show next week. Or you want to buy a new phone, a longboard, or supplies to start a business. Maybe you simply want to get started saving toward $1 million. Those probably all fall under the category of **short-term goals**.

So how do you reach your short-term goal? Figure out the cost of the goal, then divide by the amount of time you have to reach it.

Say you want some Super-Cool Thingy. The Super-Cool Thingy is $100 and you want to have it by next summer, which is 10 months away. That means you need to save $10 a month to reach your short-term goal of having

CHARTING A COURSE
FOR THE ISLAND OF FINANCIAL FREEDOM

SHORT-TERM GOALS

NOW TO 1 YEAR

MEDIUM-TERM GOALS

1 TO 10 YEARS

LONG-TERM GOALS

OVER 10 YEARS

GO!

enough money to buy the Super-Cool Thingy. Can you do it? If not, modify the goal a little. Either you need to get more money, spend less, or do some combination of the two. Another option would be to give yourself a little more time to save.

MEDIUM-TERM GOALS
(1 TO 10 YEARS)

MAYBE you want to buy a car, travel, save for college, or move out of the house by the time you're 20. These are probably more **medium-term goals**. Again, figure out how much money you need to reach the goal and divide by the time you have to reach it. Let's say a trip to Europe costs $5,000 and you want to do it in three years. Divide $5,000 by 36 months and you get about $138.89 a month. Can you set a short-term goal to save $138.89 a month, toward a medium-term goal of saving $5,000 in three years? If not, then modify the goal. Maybe plan a cheaper trip, go later, or figure out a way to bring in more money.

LONG-TERM GOALS
(OVER 10 YEARS)

THESE goals could be 10, 20, 30, 40 years, and beyond. That may seem like a long way out, but millions of people before you have had that same thought, then suddenly realized they should have started thinking about **long-term goals** when they were 11 years old! Want to retire early, travel

Keep your goals written somewhere that you'll see every day.

How to Turn $100 into $1,000,000

the world, buy a house, have kids or just lots of dogs? Sounds like you're going to need a million dollars to reach some of those goals, so these are probably long-term and ultra-long-term goals.

Let's say you want to have $1 million in 40 years. Divide $1,000,000 by 40 and you'll get $25,000 per year. We know what you're thinking. "I'm just 11 years old. I'm never going to be able to save that much!" The good news is you don't have to actually save $25,000 per year for 40 years to get to $1 million. There's a trick we'll share later where your money starts making money for you. Don't skip ahead!

WRITE THEM DOWN!

IT'S critical that your goals are clear and spell out exactly what you want. Write them down, type them up, or text them to yourself, and definitely jot them down in *Your Two-Page Plan to Become a Millionaire* on page 124 of this book. Hang them on the fridge, or post them someplace to look at every day. You're more likely to achieve them if they're written down and right in front of your face. And don't be afraid to revise your goals. They'll change over time.

TURNING JEWELRY INTO A DIRT BIKE

Christian had a passion for dirt-biking and wanted a new bike. His goal was to buy one within a year, which meant saving $50 per month for 12 months. So Christian made jewelry and sold it to friends and family, and also set up a stand at a local pizza restaurant where he sold his products on the weekends. At first Christian's friends made fun of him . . . until he showered them in mud while ripping past them on his brand-new bike!

EPIC WIN

Jim Carrey, one of the highest paid actors of all time, has earned millions for his movies. It wasn't always that way, however. In 1985, as a struggling actor trying to make it in Hollywood, Carrey drove to the top of the Hollywood Hills. While dreaming of his future, he wrote himself a check for $10 million, dated it Thanksgiving 1995, added the notation "for acting services rendered," and carried it in his wallet from that day forth.

The rest, as they say, is history. Carrey's optimism and tenacity eventually paid off, and by 1995, after several huge box-office hits, his asking price had risen to $20 million per picture. Writing down that goal of being able to pay himself $10 million helped focus Carrey's mental state for his eventual success.

So what are you doing to get the future you want? Maybe you think your current situation is the best that's possible. Could you focus your mind into expecting success even with the obstacles you think you have? Don't wait on luck, winning the lottery, or for that rich uncle to die. Decide what you want your future to be and then get busy planning it and setting goals. Maybe you need to write yourself a check and put a date on it for 20 years from now.

MONITOR YOUR PROGRESS

MAYBE you lost your job. Maybe you got a raise. Maybe that stock you invested in skyrocketed. Maybe it crashed. Even the best financial plan can hit a meltdown. Stay on top of things and check your progress on a regular basis. If you've set a short-term goal of getting that Super-Cool Thingy in a year, maybe stop and assess how you're doing every month. Maybe you'll find yourself ahead of your goals. Awesome! If not, adjust a little.

So what happens when you reach your goal? Celebrate! Then set a new goal and move on. You still have that $1 million to aim for.

WHAT'S THE POINT?

ALL of us dream of things we'd like to do in the future and what we'd like our lives to become. You will have the best chance of reaching those dreams if you set goals, write them down, and then plan on how to get there. Having a plan with a set of financial goals is the foundation for your financial future.

LONG STORY SHORT

1. If you want to make $1 million, set short-, medium-, and long-term goals.

2. Write down your goals.

3. Monitor your progress, and adjust if necessary.

Chapter 3:
MAKE A BUDGET

HAVE you ever tried to get someplace new without first looking up directions? It isn't easy or very smart. Well, if you're going to successfully reach any short-, medium-, or long-term financial goals, you'll need directions.

A budget is your financial road map. It's going to take you from where you're sitting right now to millionaire-land.

A budget is a tool to help you live within your means. It's a snapshot of all the money that comes in (**income**) and

EPIC BUDGET FAIL

G'day mate! While the Sydney Opera House is an iconic building and a global symbol of Australia, it's also seen as one of the biggest budget blunders in modern history. Construction on the project started in 1959 after the Danish architect Jørn Utzon won the Australian government's architecture competition. The project was scheduled to take four years, with a budget of AUS $7 million. It ended up taking 14 years to complete and cost AUS $102 million. Now that's blowing the budget almost 15 times over! Yikes!

all the money that goes out (**expenses**). As the money comes and goes, you refer to your budget to see how you're doing with your spending and saving. Think of it as a game with a goal to stay within your budget.

BUILDING A BETTER BUDGET

MAKING a budget is not really that hard. For a monthly budget, you just estimate your monthly income and compare that to your monthly expenses. Your income may include things like an allowance, a paycheck,

A budget blunder down under!

cash gifts, loans, or interest from savings accounts and investment **portfolios**. Expenses are all the things you pay for during the month—like food, entertainment, clothes, any school supplies, and so on. List every expense you can think of and account for every single penny. That's why receipts are important. Save and enter them into your budget. Most people never do this, and simple purchases can be forgotten pretty fast.

If you find, after creating your budget, that your expenses are more than your income, there are only two things you can do:

1. INCREASE YOUR INCOME.

2. CUT BACK ON EXPENSES.

Did we say two things? Here's a third:

3. DO A LITTLE OF BOTH.

Let's say you want to start off on your journey toward $1 million. You have a

short-term goal to reach a total of $100 by saving $10 a month. With a budget, you'll know where all the money goes. You'll see your income and spending patterns, which can be tweaked and adjusted to help you reach your goal of saving $10 per month.

List every expense, especially those new skateboard shoes you bought, in your budget.

KEEP IT SIMPLE

A budget doesn't have to be complicated. Keep it simple. Don't spend more than you earn and don't forget that chunk of money you are going to put aside every month toward your goal of reaching $1 million. As your budget expands, you should add a separate budget line for an emergency fund that is separate from your million-dollar fund. Impress your parents when *(Continued on page 23)*

YOUR MONTHLY BUDGET

This is what a monthly budget might look like for you. Let's say last week you got a monthly allowance of $20, made $20 from a quick babysitting gig, and—surprise—got a birthday gift from Granny for $5. That total is $45. Great. Put that down under "Income."

YOUR MONTHLY BUDGET
SEPTEMBER

INCOME		
WEEK 1	Allowance	$20
	Babysitting	$20
	Gift	$5

Maybe you won't be making $45 each week. Maybe your income will fluctuate. Most weeks you won't get $5 from Granny. Other weeks you might sell a couple of used games or do some extra chores. Estimate your income for the next month; be conservative. Let's say you're ambitious and bring in around $100 per month.

YOUR MONTHLY BUDGET
SEPTEMBER

INCOME		
WEEK 1	Allowance	$20
	Babysitting	$20
	Gift	$5
WEEK 2	No Income	$0
WEEK 3	Sell Games	$30
WEEK 4	Extra Chores	$25
TOTAL	$100	

Next list all the expenses you think you'll have that month, including that goal of saving $10 a month. Even though your savings goals are not an expense, they should be included in the list and paid first. That's called **Pay Yourself First (PYF)**, and it's a great strategy to make sure the money intended for your savings account hits the bank before you spend it! Financial bigwigs say that you'll never make your savings goals unless you do this *first*.

After that, list things like lunch, your cell phone bill, new shoes, movie tickets, a video game, and paying your little sister back for the money she lent you. List every expense. It's great if you also have a receipt for the expense so you'll remember the right amount. Your expected expenses will be a little different from your actual expenses, which is why you want to update your budget throughout the month. And again, don't leave anything out. Track your expenses each week to see how they compare to your monthly budget. If expenses total more than income, you're going to blow your budget. Something will have to wait until you bring in more income or cut your expenses. At least now you can figure out which of those expenses is a priority.

Let's say for this month the new shoes and the movie will have to wait.

YOUR MONTHLY BUDGET
SEPTEMBER

INCOME		
WEEK 1	Allowance	$20
	Babysitting	$20
	Gift	$5
WEEK 2	No Income	$0
WEEK 3	Sell Games	$30
WEEK 4	Extra Chores	$25
TOTAL	$100	

EXPENSES		
WEEK 1	Savings Account	$10
	Cell Phone Bill (split with parents)	$10
WEEK 2	Movie Tickets	$16
WEEK 3	Lunch	$28.03
	Skateboard Wheels	$42.77
WEEK 4	Pay Back Sister	$2
	Shoes	$110
TOTAL	$218.80	
TOTAL INCOME LESS TOTAL EXPENSES	−$118.80	
	BUDGET BLOWN!	

Here's what your final budget for September might look like:

YOUR MONTHLY BUDGET
SEPTEMBER

INCOME	EXPECTED		ACTUAL	
WEEK 1	Allowance	$20	Allowance	$20
	Babysitting	$20	Babysitting	$20
			Gift	$5
WEEK 2	No Income	$0	No Income	$0
WEEK 3	Sell Games	$30	Sell Games	$30
WEEK 4	No Income	$0	Extra Chores	$25
TOTAL	$70		$100	

EXPENSES	EXPECTED		ACTUAL	
WEEK 1	Savings Account	$10	Savings Account	$10
	Cell Phone (split with parents)	$10	Cell Phone (split with parents)	$10
WEEK 2	Movie Tickets	$16		
WEEK 3	Lunch	$28.03	Lunch	$28.03
	Skateboard Wheels	$42.77	Skateboard Wheels	$42.77
WEEK 4	Pay Back Sister	$2	Pay Back Sister	$2
	Shoes	$110		
TOTAL	$218.80		$92.80	
TOTAL INCOME LESS TOTAL EXPENSES	−$118.80		$7.20	
	BUDGET BLOWN!		BUDGET MADE!	

(Continued from page 19)
you tell them most experts agree you should have three to six months' worth of income set aside for a potential crisis.

When you're just starting off, money will be tight and you'll have to make some trade-offs. Maybe you pack a lunch instead of eating out or watch a movie at home instead of heading to the theater. Bam! You just saved $25 by sticking to your budget. A lot of times the adjustment can be minimal, with a small sacrifice but a big payoff.

Your budget won't be perfect at the beginning. You'll be constantly adjusting it. Work on it every day for three months and see what happens. Keep going for six months and see what it does for your financial future. Knowing how to budget will be a gift that sticks with you for the rest of your life.

BUDGETING WITH CASH

When sticking to a budget, nothing beats using cold hard cash. Put money in an envelope labeled with the type of expense. For example, if you want to spend $30 a month on entertainment, put $30 in an envelope, and write "entertainment" on top. Use the money inside to purchase whatever you consider entertainment. Once it's gone, it's gone, until the next month. If there's any cash leftover, leave it in the envelope for next month or put it into your savings.

LONG STORY SHORT

1. *A budget will help you reach your financial goals.*

2. *If your budget is blown, you need to either increase income, decrease expenses, or do a little of both.*

3. *To meet your savings goals, Pay Yourself First!*

Chapter 4:
FIVE WAYS TO GET MONEY

YOU need money to make money. So, where do you get your first dollar? That should be pretty easy. You can simply ask somebody for $1. You could even ask for $10 and see what they say. Ask them for $100 and you might get a totally different response.

But let's start by setting a short-term goal of getting $100. Why? Because that's the title of this book: *How to Turn $100 into $1,000,000*. From $100 the long-term goal should be $1 million. That's a big leap, we know. But if you can get $100, you can get $1 million. Trust us.

THE FIVE WAYS

THERE are five ways you can reach your short-term goal and get your hands on $100.

1. GET AN ALLOWANCE.

According to *Time* magazine, 61% of American parents give their children an allowance. Maybe you're in that majority. Maybe you get an allowance in exchange for doing chores or as a way for you to learn about money. If so, that's great because saving part of your allowance is an easy way to get started on the road to financial freedom.

How much should you save? Depends on the allowance. Let's see now, what was our short-term goal? To save $100 in 10 months? The average allowance American parents pay their kids, across all age groups, is $65 per month. If that's about what you get and you saved it all, you'd have your $100 in a month and a half! But again, that's if you saved all of it, which is probably not practical. If you get a bigger allowance than that, set your goal a little higher than $100. If you

get a smaller allowance, no worries; it just might take a little longer to reach your goal.

Whatever amount you get, here are two things you can do to maximize the power of your allowance:

- **ASK FOR A RAISE.** Just as adults do with their jobs, you can ask for more money—but you better have a good reason ready. "Hey, Mom, can I have more money?" is not as effective as, "Hey, Mom, I'll add walking the dog to my list of chores if you'll up my allowance by $1 per week." Always ask for a reasonable amount and provide a justification for it.

• **SAVE, SPEND, AND SHARE.** What do you do when you get your allowance? Blow it all at the mall? Well, that's just one thing you can do—spend it. But there are actually three things you can do with your allowance: save it, spend it, or share it.

Before you get your allowance, decide how much you are going to dedicate to each of these three categories, and have containers for each. Maybe it's three mason jars, three piggy banks, or three dirty socks. We don't care—as long as you put a label on each one for save, spend, and share. If you can decide ahead of time, *before* you get your allowance, how to divide up your money, then your chances of meeting your goal of saving $100 will happen in no time.

Just make sure to put the money you want to save in a **bank** or **credit union** ASAP. A stinky sock is no place for your future $1 million. See Chapter 7 for more savings info.

The save, spend, and share sock system.

ASK YOUR PARENTS FOR A RAISE

Dear [Fill in Name Here],

I, [insert name], your [first son / third daughter / middle child, etc.] respectfully request you consider raising my monthly allowance by [insert $ amount or %]. While I sincerely appreciate my current generous monthly stipend, it's simply not enough to address my financial goal of becoming a millionaire by the time I'm [insert age]. The reasons for the increase are as follows:

1.

2.

3.

Thank you for your consideration.

Respectfully yours,
[Sign your name here]

NO ALLOWANCE?

No worries. Again, first ask for one. Have you tried that? A lot of kids need to bring up the subject of an allowance. Maybe it's just a dollar to start. Maybe it doesn't have to come on a regular basis. Most of the time, it won't hurt to ask. Here's a way to ask for an allowance that will help get results:

Dear [Fill in the Blank],
I'm starting to learn about money and how to be financially independent. I want to build my economic future and would like to start receiving a monthly allow-ance. An allowance will help me reach my short-term goal of saving $100 in 10 months.

You might need to add:

"In exchange for my allowance I would be willing to help out more around the house. I know you've asked me to help in the past and I didn't do my best. This time I'm serious. Believe me, I'll remember this when I'm a millionaire.

Tried that and no luck? Maybe an allowance just doesn't work for your family's budget. No problem. Move on to a second way you can get money.

2. WORK FOR IT.

Another way to get money is to work for it. We know, work for money? What a crazy concept.

The ways you can work for money are pretty much limited only by your imagination. Maybe you already have to work to get an allowance. Do you take out the trash? Feed the animals?

Ironing your dad's boxers might stink, but hey, it's money in the bank.

Vacuum the house? Maybe it's time to work more. Maybe it's time to start a business. We talk a lot more about jobs and starting your own business in later chapters of this book, but here are a few tips to get you started.

- **START SMALL.** Think of extra jobs you could do around the house (most likely after your regular chores are done). You could paint that peeling garden shed. Pull up weeds in the parking strip. Iron your dad's underwear (easy on the starch). There are probably lots of jobs your parents would give you a few bucks to do.

- **ASK AROUND.** Ask friends and neighbors if they have any jobs you could do. Yard care, dog walking, and babysitting are classic kid jobs, but think outside the box—you can also offer to organize, paint, or sweep your way to your first $100.

In fact, working for the $100 might be faster than saving up your allowance month after month (if you get an allowance at all). Plus, it also gives you valuable skills that you can use to get work when you reach the age required in your state to get a "real" job (i.e., be legally employed). We talk more about that in chapter 5!

3. GET A GIFT.

Remember we said you can ask for money? Did it work? Well, sometimes people will just *give* you money as a gift. From $5 from Grandma to $50 in graduation gifts, you should factor that money as "Income" in your budget and apply some of that toward your goal of the million.

We know what you're thinking. *Dude, I gotta blow some of it! Does it have to be all of the money?* No. But move a good chunk of that cash into your **savings account** and tell the gift giver how you are applying some of it toward your long-term goal of saving $1 million. And who knows? Maybe they'll be so impressed they'll give you more next time.

Another type of gift is called an **inheritance**. Almost everyone dreams of suddenly coming into money. That rich friend or relative who unfortunately dies, but fortunately leaves you with a tidy sum of millions. C'mon, admit it.

The thought has crossed your mind. You've seen the movie:

Dear So-and-So,

Your beloved uncle, Lord Sir Reginald What's-His-Name, fell from a parapet and was impaled on a crumpet fork. Our greatest condolences to you. Given that you have never heard of him, you may not feel his loss as keenly as does his cat Mittens. As his last surviving heir, you shall inherit his castle, his collection of Ferraris, $1 billion, and one slightly bent crumpet fork. However, in order to satisfy the conditions of the will, you must swim the English Channel and take care of Mittens for the rest of her natural life. Please respond at your earliest convenience.

There's always a catch, isn't there?

Anytime you get a gift or an unexpected **windfall** it's tempting to think about all the stuff you could buy. Maybe new clothes. Maybe a car! Maybe . . . Uh-oh, we're losing you to financial fantasy! Activate financial reality!

That's why you use your budget as your anchor to keep you from financially drifting when you get an unexpected chunk of change—whether it's $10 or $100. Heck, maybe the gift is more than $100! Woo-hoo! Now, you've already reached that first short-term goal and you just got started. Put that money in a savings account today. Now. Yesterday! Then set another short-term goal of $500.

WHAT'S-HIS-NAME

4. BORROW IT.

A fourth way to get money is to borrow it. Borrowing money is tricky and, generally speaking, a bad idea when you're just starting out. People who lend you money (the **lender**) will want something in return from you (the **borrower**). That's called **interest** (usually expressed as a percentage of the amount you borrowed). If you want to buy something big, like a house, this can be very useful. But if you want to turn $100 into $1 million, you might consider other options. We suggest not borrowing money until you are well educated in the ways of debt and **credit**.

5. EARN INTEREST ON INVESTMENTS.

This is one of the most effective ways to save up $1 million.

When you make an investment with a financial institution or deposit your money in a savings account, you'll be paid interest. An investment is something you purchase with the expectation it will generate income (such as interest) or go up in value in the future. When you earn interest on your investments, your money is working for you, without you having to do much but keep an eye on your investment. It's a great way for kids to make money because you can be off doing something else, like riding your bike.

Your first step should be to put money in a savings account at a bank or credit union. You will earn very little interest by keeping your money in this account, but it is a great place to build up the cash necessary to move into other investments that will pay you much higher interest, such as certificates of deposit, **stocks**, **bonds**, a new business. The list goes on and on.

6. STEAL IT.

Don't do it. That's why we say there are only five ways to earn money.

This guy isn't getting a million bucks anytime soon.

MONEY MOMENT

Now that you know the ways to get money, let's figure out if they bring in "passive" or "active" income. "Active" income means you physically work for the money. "Passive" income is money that comes in without much work needed to generate it. You might have to put in a bunch of effort up front, but then it requires only a little bit of ongoing maintenance.

Passive income can include interest from savings, stocks, and other investments. But it can also include income from a business that can run itself most of the time, such as a vending machine, selling items on eBay, rent from real estate, and so on. You can even develop a blog, YouTube channel, or a podcast and earn money from ads, if you can attract enough viewers. The great thing about "passive" income for kids is you don't need to keep bugging your parents or an older sibling to drive you anywhere to earn some money—you can just sit in your pajamas at home and watch the cash roll in.

RINSE AND REPEAT!

OKAY, let's say that by using the five ways to get money, you've made your short-term goal of getting $100 in your savings account. Congratulations! You're on your way to $1 million! All you do now is rinse and repeat. Modify your goals to go for $200, then $500, then $1,000, then $5,000, and then a major benchmark—$10,000! When you've finally got some money to work with, you can initiate a secret money-making accelerator that we'll talk about in chapter 8. It will blow your mind.

For now, just bask in the glow of getting to $100.

Oh, one more thing:

GOT THAT MONEY IN A SAVINGS ACCOUNT?

 Check.

ENTER IT AS INCOME IN YOUR BUDGET?

 Check.

STARTING TO LIKE THIS?

 Check.

MAKING MONEY IN MORE THAN ONE WAY

Thirteen-year-old twins Ethan and Jacqueline already got an allowance. . . but it just wasn't enough. Ethan wanted to save up for an iPod, and Jacqueline needed more spending money. So they started a business—a tennis and craft summer camp for kids. Ethan taught tennis while Jacqueline taught crafts. Being creative about how to get money served them well—by the end of the summer they'd met their goal!

LONG STORY SHORT

1. There are five ways to make money: allowance, work, gifts, loans, and interest on investments.

2. To earn $1 million, you have to start small—set a goal of making $100.

3. Don't steal it. Ever. Making $1 million is impossible if you're behind bars.

Chapter 5:
GET A JOB!

IF your main goal is to amass $1 million, at some point, your allowance (if you are lucky enough to get one) isn't going to cut the mustard. You'll need a faster way to get more money to save and invest over time.

One of the fastest ways to get money is to have a job. A few lucky individuals can just fall into a job or have one handed to them. For most of us, however, finding a job requires a lot of work.

The good news is that a job is not

only a great way to get money now, but it also gives you valuable experience to make *more* money in the future—even if all you learn is that you *don't* want to clean horse trailers for a living. (Our apologies to those who like to clean horse trailers for a living.) There are thousands of first jobs out there that you can choose from. Most will be close to cleaning horse trailers (again, our apologies)—the lowest jobs on the ladder. We're talking hamburger flipping, taco stuffing, bathroom cleaning, roof ripping, eel wrestling. . .

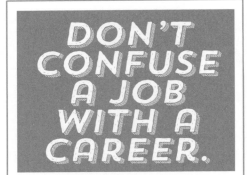

Which leads us to this: Don't be confused between a job and a **career**. Your first job probably will not be your career. There are exceptions: You could start as an intern at a gaming company and end up spending the rest of your life in the industry. But no one is going to hand you the keys to their business on the first day. You need to show that you can handle the most basic responsibilities and demonstrate follow-through to gain trust. And get this: You need to *work hard*. It's a proving ground for the employer to know if you can handle the work. But, for now, let's focus on getting that first job.

This requires a little strategy. First, ask yourself what you are interested in doing. Making money is always first on that list, but what are you truly passionate about? What industry or business excites you?

Maybe you have dreams of owning your own restaurant. Get a job as a dishwasher, then quickly fill in for a server who's sick. Soon you have a server's job. Two years later, you take over as manager. Maybe you stay, or maybe you become a manager at a different restaurant. Hey, you're moving up the ladder. You'll probably work at a few jobs (and even try a few different industries) before you land the perfect gig.

"GET A JOB" MASTER PLAN

HERE are the typical steps in finding a job—we'll cover them all in the upcoming pages:

1. Decide what job you want.

2. Find an open job.

3. Apply for the job.

4. Get an interview (or several).

5. Keep at it! Repeat steps 1 to 4 until you get hired.

1. DECIDE WHAT JOB YOU WANT.

ONE of the first things you should do is put together a list of potential jobs that you can do. Brain surgery is probably out. So is running the World Bank. What can *you* do? Don't say "nothing." Everybody can do something. Go ahead, think about it for a minute . . .

Okay, time's up! Here are some ways to figure out which jobs might be right for you:

- **DIVIDE A PIECE OF PAPER IN HALF.** List your skills and strengths on one side.

CLASSIC FIRST JOBS

These classic first jobs are often called entry-level jobs, and they're just what they sound like—your "entry" into the world of money:

Babysitter, lawn mower and landscaper, pizza delivery person, restaurant server or dishwasher, pooper scooper, fast-food worker, farm worker, stocker and bagger at a grocery store, mail room sorter, stable worker, mechanic's assistant, dog walker, golf caddy, house painter, lifeguard, music instructor, tutor, gym towel folder, theater concessions attendant, computer repairer, valet at a car park, cherry picker, asparagus harvester, horse trailer cleaner, gas station cashier, car wash attendant, errand runner for the elderly, etc.

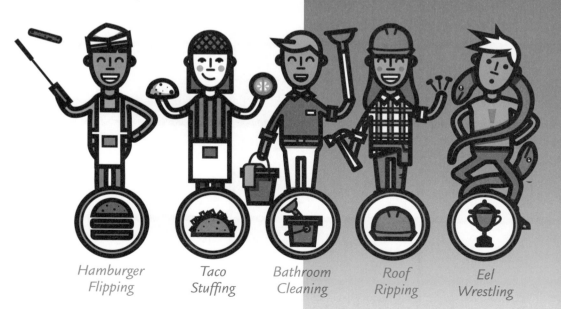

Hamburger Flipping *Taco Stuffing* *Bathroom Cleaning* *Roof Ripping* *Eel Wrestling*

EIGHT BILLIONAIRES AND THEIR FIRST JOBS

Everyone has to start somewhere—even these billionaires. Notice how none of them had glamorous jobs to start with. They worked their way up, just like everyone else.

BILLIONAIRE	COMPANY	FIRST JOB
Jeff Bezos	Founder, Amazon.com	Worked the grill at McDonald's
Oprah Winfrey	Founder, Harpo Productions	Stocked shelves at a grocery store
Michael Dell	Founder, Dell Computers	Washed dishes at a Chinese restaurant
Charles Schwab	Founder, Charles Schwab Corporation	Collected walnuts found in the woods and sold them at $5 per 100-pound bag
Michael Bloomberg	Founder, Bloomberg, LP, and former mayor of New York City	Worked as a car parking lot attendant
Sara Blakely	Founder, Spanx	Donned mouse ears at Disney World, guiding patrons onto a ride at Epcot Center
Barry Diller	Chairman, IAC/InterActiveCorp and Expedia, Inc.	Started in the mail room at the William Morris Agency, and eventually became head of Paramount Studios
Warren Buffett	CEO, Berkshire Hathaway	Delivered newspapers on his bike at 13

List your interests on the other. Think about what kind of job might play to both. Do you enjoy interacting with people? Retail or food service could be a great choice. Love animals? Look into pet sitting or assisting at a veterinary hospital.

• **ASK AROUND.** Talk to family and friends. What kind of work did they do when they were young? You might be surprised at the answers, and this may inspire you to look for a job you never thought of.

• **VOLUNTEER.** Helping out at different types of charitable organizations is a great way

WHEN CAN I START?

As a general rule, 14 years of age is the minimum age for employment in America, but most **state labor laws** require you to be 15 or 16 years old. There are also limits to the number of hours you can work and rules that may prevent you from doing certain jobs until you are 18 or older. These include jobs that are hazardous—like running a nuclear power plant, operating chain saws, or driving a taxicab.

(Continued on page 40)

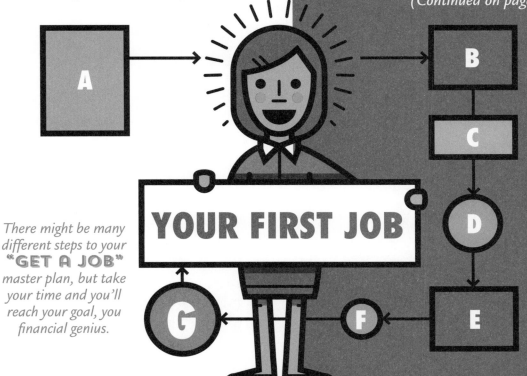

There might be many different steps to your **"GET A JOB"** *master plan, but take your time and you'll reach your goal, you financial genius.*

It's pretty easy to look up the laws for your state online, and most employers have this info as well. There are exceptions to the rules. For example, you might be able to work for your parents in a family-run business.

NOT MINIMUM AGE YET?

You can always work for a friend or a neighbor, if you can agree on a job and an hourly rate. Maybe you let the cat out every day for a family next door. Maybe you rake leaves for people on the block. Maybe you detail cars. We know a young kid who was too young for regular employment, so she started her own dog-walking business. If being a young business tycoon is something you find appealing, you can learn how to start your own business in chapter 6.

to gain skills, try new jobs, and see what fits your interests.

• **CONSIDER YOUR NATURAL ABILITIES.** Are you an early riser or a night owl? Funny or serious? Always on time or constantly running behind? Think about jobs that might suit your personality best.

There are also **internships** offered at thousands of companies across the country. Internships usually are unpaid positions, but in exchange you get great work experience and get your foot in the door at some pretty amazing businesses.

2. FIND AN OPEN JOB.

THE next step is to find a job that's open—meaning they are actively looking for someone to fill it. There are several places to find open jobs.

• **FAMILY & FRIENDS.** Talking to the folks you know is *the* best place to start. So get the word out! Tell everyone you know that you're looking for a job. Definitely talk to people who work at places you like

*Are you a pet person? Volunte
at a shelter or animal hospit*

and find out if they hire young people. You'll have a built-in recommendation!

• **JOB LISTINGS.** Search job posting sites in your area, and you'll get lots of results in a fifth of a second, or try local message boards. You can also still find classified ads in your local newspaper. Have a trusted adult help you with any job search and never go to an interview without having thoroughly checked out who your potential employer is. *Never* go to an interview alone.

• **JUST WALK IN.** At many restaurants and retailers, you can just walk in and ask for a job application.

• **BUSINESS WEBSITE.** If you want to work for a specific company, you can see if they have an application on their website. This is especially common with fast-food chains and retailers.

3. APPLY FOR THE JOB.

ONCE you find an open job, you'll have to fill out an application, provide a résumé, or both.

Here's some information you should have with you when you're going to apply for a job, in case you have to complete an application form on the spot:

• **PERSONAL INFO,** including your Social Security number, address, contact info, etc.

• **OTHER JOBS YOU'VE HAD,** including any past responsibilities, dates of employment, and past employer contact info. You can include volunteer work here, too.

• **REFERENCES**, meaning people the employer can call to find out if you are trustworthy. The best **references** are former employers, but you can also use coaches, teachers, or other adults who know you well. Avoid using friends or family members. Employers don't want a reference from your mom.

MAKE A RÉSUMÉ!

LET'S say you want a job as a babysitter or bagger at a grocery store. The person who would hire you will want to know who you are. A **résumé** is a one-page story of your work or business experience—an advertisement for why someone should hire you. Even if you don't need one for the jobs you're applying for, it's a great exercise to put one together.

Make sure your résumé looks professional. Also, you don't have to give the same résumé to every employer. You can tweak it for different jobs.

WHAT'S IN A GOOD RÉSUMÉ?

NAME AND CONTACT INFORMATION. Put your name, mailing address, phone number, and email address at the top of the page. Make sure your email address isn't immature or offensive—if yours is partydude@lazymail.com, you might want to get a new one just for job applications.

OBJECTIVE. This tells the employer what kind of job you are looking for. Don't be afraid to advertise your skills here a little. You can just put it in your own words like this:

> OBJECTIVE:
> Seeking employment in the food service industry to demonstrate superior people skills.

You can change the objective to reflect who's reading your résumé. If it's a golf course, change the objective to say something like "seeking employment in the golf industry." If it's a grocery store, say something like "seeking employment in the food and retail business."

EDUCATION. List the schools you've attended. You don't have to go back to pre-K, but you should list the name of your current school or any other relevant classes you've taken, including the dates when you took them. For example, if you are applying to work in day care, you could mention babysitting classes. If you are trying to get a job in a music store, make sure you list band or orchestra class. Also include any awards of recognition or the honor roll.

WORK EXPERIENCE. You probably have more experience than you think. List any paid, unpaid, or volunteer experience. Let's say you are applying at a landscaping business— maybe you list experience mowing neighbors' yards or caring for plants. When listing your experience, make sure that the most applicable experience is listed first.

OTHER SKILLS. These are the additional skills that make you a good candidate for the job. It could include specific software knowledge or skills acquired through volunteer jobs. If you are applying at a grocery store, maybe you have experience volunteering at a food bank stocking shelves. If you volunteered at an animal shelter, list that on your résumé when applying to a veterinary clinic. If you are applying to be a lifeguard or babysitter, and have taken CPR training, list it. You might also include points like hard worker, self-motivated, or good with people.

HOBBIES & INTERESTS. This is not the most important part of a résumé but an employer is always curious about your interests. It can be a great point of connection during the interview. If you ski, make sure you list it, particularly if you are applying for a job at a ski area. Do your friends ask you to fix their computers? Mention that here. Don't forget club memberships, extracurricular awards, or scholarships.

REFERENCES. Many potential employers ask for references. You can either list them on your résumé or write "References available on request." It is very important to check with your references in advance to make sure it's okay for employers to contact them.

CHECK YOUR WORK!

- **PROOFREAD.** Once you have written your résumé, make sure there are no spelling mistakes or grammatical errors (don't rely on spell-checker!). One mistake can make the difference between getting the job or losing it.

- **SIMPLIFY.** Avoid freaky fonts or crazy colors. Keep it simple and spend your energy on what the résumé actually says.

- **UPDATE.** Rarely are résumés perfect on the very first pass. They should constantly be tweaked, added to, and adjusted.

- **NEVER LIE.** *Never!* If you don't have any relevant experience, don't make it up!

4. GET AN INTERVIEW.

YOU wouldn't hire somebody without getting to know them a little better, would you? Neither would anyone else. So if you want the job, you should know how to ace an interview. Everybody is nervous during a **job interview**. Everybody! But you can be less nervous if you are prepared.

DRESS FOR SUCCESS

Want to score that first gig? The clothes you wear to school or the mall aren't likely to cut it in an interview. Toss the gum, keep good eye contact, and relax. If you remember that first impressions count, you'll be able to count on that first paycheck!

Clean, well-groomed hair and no hats

Avoid large and too much jewelry

T-shirts not appropriate for most jobs

Avoid jeans or too-short skirts

Dress for success from head to toe, so no flip-flops, sneakers or combat boots

Yes!   *No!*   *No!*   *Yes!*

SAMPLE RÉSUMÉ

The actual format of a résumé isn't set in stone. We've given you a guide. Now it's time to make it your own. Here is a sample résumé to get you started.

Ellie McKenna

421 Eastern Road, Ardsley, NY 10530 • Home: 111.111.1111 • Cell: 444.444.4444 • ellie@youremail.com

OBJECTIVE

Interested in a paid summer day camp position working up to 15 hours per week.

EDUCATION

Central Ardsley School—Ardsley, NY   (write dates of attendance here)
Activities: Band and Stage Crew
Awards: Honor Roll

SPECIAL SKILLS and INTERESTS

* Love to work with children
* Can create attractive posters and flyers using graphic software
* Good with Microsoft Word, Excel, and PowerPoint
* Manage family recycling assignments
* Play bass guitar
* Enjoy reading plays and the biographies of famous people

VOLUNTEER and COMMUNITY SERVICE

Bainbridge Hospital, Ardsley, NY
Pediatric Ward Volunteer   (write dates here)
* Occupied children by reading books and playing games
* Made sure the play area was neat and toys were put away after use
* Ran errands or completed assignments for staff

Ardsley Recreation Department, City of Ardsley, NY
Volunteer Day Camp Counselor in Training   (write dates here)
* Led arts, crafts, sports, games, camping, and hobby workshops for groups of five- to eight-year-olds
* Made sure campers were dropped off and picked up safely

GOALS

* Plan to study psychology or music as a major in college
* Join the Pep Squad in next year

And remember, with many employers you can submit a résumé even if they don't have open positions at the moment. Many keep résumés on file and call promising candidates when jobs open up. So apply early and follow up often!

EPIC WIN EPIC FAIL EPIC WIN

Losing your job is not the end of the world—in fact it could mean a new beginning. Case in point, Steve Jobs created Apple Computers when he was just 20 years old. Ten years later, Jobs was forced out of his own company by the board of directors. After his exit Jobs founded NeXT, which ended up developing the software used for Mac OS X, 10 years down the road. Jobs also launched Pixar, which went on to produce many animated box-office hits, like *Toy Story*, *Finding Nemo*, *Inside Out*, and more. Then, 12 years after his departure from Apple, Jobs returned to become CEO and helped reinvent and reinvigorate the company.

Here are a few interview tips:

• **DO HOMEWORK.** Do some research on the business. Find out all you can about what goods or services it provides. That will make it easier to talk about what value you can add, and how you'll be a great employee.

• **PRACTICE.** Go online and research common interview questions and answers. Then do a practice interview with a friend or relative. Have this person ask you five or six sample questions. Learn to confidently answer in short, articulate sentences.

• **BE CURIOUS.** During the interview, ask questions about the company. Are they planning on expanding? What products or services would they like to offer in the future that they do not offer now? Ask where they see themselves in five years. It may seem a bit awkward, but they will be impressed. It means you're interested in helping make their company a success.

• **BE CONFIDENT.** Look the interviewer in the eye and greet the interviewer with a firm handshake. Even if you're nervous, act like you're not! Answer questions honestly, but be brief. You don't want to say just yes or no, but you also don't want to go on and on about your trip through the Canadian Rockies.

• **FOLLOW UP!** After the interview, send a nice thank-you email to the interviewer. If you really want to impress them, send a handwritten note. And don't be afraid to follow up in a week or two. Here's an example note:

Ms. Jones,

Thank you for taking the time to meet with me regarding the position of Summer Production Assistant. By hiring me, Financial Films will get a passionate, hardworking employee. I believe my skills would be a valuable asset to the company. If you need more information, please don't hesitate to let me know. I look forward to hearing from you soon.

Sincerely,

Marshawn

5. KEEP AT IT!

IF you don't get the job—don't despair. Most people who are looking for work apply to several places before they get hired. The secret is to keep at it. Sometimes it's good to get feedback on why you didn't get the job. Don't hesitate to follow up and find out how you could do better, where you did well, or where you fell short. Sharpen up your skills. Polish your résumé. **Be persistent** and someone will eventually say "Congratulations, you got the job."

NOW WHAT? KEEPING THE JOB YOU HAVE.

ONCE you start a new job, you have to prove that you're worth keeping. Here are a few tips to help you stand out in a good way:

• **LOOK SMART.** Looking sharp shows you take your work seriously. If you wear a uniform, make sure it's clean. If there's a dress code, follow it.

- **BE ON TIME.** They're paying you for your time and they expect to get it! Arrive early and you'll definitely get noticed.

- **LISTEN, WATCH, AND LEARN.** Pay attention to people who have been doing the job longer than you have—they can provide valuable information.

- **GET INTO IT.** Find ways to improve your skills, help out when you have extra time, and put a little elbow grease into everything you do.

- **SPEAK UP.** After a while, you'll probably have good ideas for how to make things work better. Don't be afraid to share them.

- **BE HONEST.** A lot of companies have tools, supplies, products, and equipment that may be tempting to "borrow." Don't even think about it.

- **TAKE THE LEAD.** Your boss will definitely notice if you volunteer first for any project assignment.

- **CHECK IN.** Don't be afraid to ask your boss how you're doing and how you might improve.

Getting your first paycheck will make you feel like a million bucks—even if you're only making $100!

YOU'RE ON YOUR WAY!

So you have the job, and you have some income. Congratulations! Hopefully your new gig is a great fit and you can't wait to start walking those doggies, mowing those lawns, or flipping those burgers. Check back with your plan, goals, and budget to start saving as much of that money as you can.

A lot of employers offer **direct deposit** of your paycheck into a bank account. Do it! Getting that first paycheck will make you feel rich, and you'll be tempted to spend it all. Your savings account is just a little way to help you manage your money, instead of blowing everything. Hey, you worked for it. Don't just toss it away. Keeping that money safely tucked away will have you well on your way to earning $1 million! Bon voyage!

LONG STORY SHORT

1. Getting a job is the fastest way to earn cash toward your million-dollar goal.

2. Figure out what kind of job you want, find an open position, write a résumé, apply, and prepare for an interview.

3. Once you get the job, kick butt and lock away part of your paycheck in a savings account.

Chapter 6:
START A BUSINESS

THINK of some rich people. I mean really rich. Like Bill Gates rich. Private islands. Caviar omelets. Yachts made of gold. How did they get that way? Did they just save their allowance? Clip coupons? Buy Florida swampland? Nope, nope, and triple nope. What they did was start businesses.

Don't get us wrong; jobs are great. You get a regular paycheck, your boss tells you what to do, and you don't have to put in any of your own money. (And you might get to wear a paper hat.)

Starting a business is totally different. There's no paycheck, no boss, and you take all the risk. So, what's the upside? Why, money, of course! Big, heaping piles of money!

Well, not *really*. But the **profit potential** from starting a successful business is greater than almost anything else you can do. It is also a great way to lose money. There are so many things that can go wrong. However, if you *really* want to make money to save up to $1 million, it's something to seriously consider.

WHY START NOW?

EVEN if you don't make $1 million on your very first try, here are six fantastic reasons to start a business now before you get all old and wrinkly.

1. IT'S AWESOME.
There's nothing like the feeling of taking an idea, making it real, and watching it grow.

2. MAKE BIG MONEY.
Starting your own business is one of the best ways to turn $100 into $1 million.

Once you come up with a profitable idea, the sky's the limit.

3. THERE'S NO TIME LIKE THE PRESENT.
Seriously. There's *no* time like being a kid. Grown-ups have all kinds of responsibilities that make it harder for them to take risks. Plus, people will think you're cute, which will help you sell them more stuff.

4. BE YOUR OWN BOSS.
Nobody likes being bossed around. But everyone likes *being* the boss. Of course, until you can get some employees, you'll only be bossing yourself around. Make sure to hire a sibling ASAP.

5. FAIL BIG.
Behind every successful businessperson is a list of blunders they made on the way to the top. You have the chance to get those out of the way early before anyone is paying attention and to learn from your mistakes.

6. LOOK SMART.
Being a business owner looks great on college applications or on a résumé. It shows initiative, smarts, and responsibility.

CAN KIDS REALLY START A BUSINESS?

Having your own business can be awesome, and kids do it all the time before they even have a driver's license. These young entrepreneurs all made their millions in different ways. One thing they had in common? They found a need and took action at an early age.

When Maddie Bradshaw, 10, wanted to decorate her locker, she couldn't find any good magnets, so she decided to make her own. With $300 of her own money and a unique idea, Maddie created Snap Caps, magnets made from bottle caps. Soon, she decided it would be fun to wear and trade her bottle caps as necklaces. With the help of her little sister, Margot, and their mother, they turned Snap Caps into a national brand, selling 50,000 necklaces per month in less than two years.

At the age of 6, Farrah Gray started selling body lotion. At thirteen he founded Farr-Out Foods, which generated over $1.5 million in sales in the first year, making him a millionaire! Since then Farrah has launched inner-city entrepreneurship programs, published books, is a motivational speaker, and sits on the board of numerous companies. Farrah was the youngest person to have an office on Wall Street.

At 17, Nick D'Aloisio set the Internet on fire when it was announced that Yahoo agreed to buy a smartphone app he created for a whopping $30 million. Nick taught himself how to code at twelve—a skill that paid off when he finally created "Summly," the news app that grabbed Yahoo's attention.

Jon Koon would look through his dad's car magazines from Japan and wonder why no one in America was dressing up their cars with special parts or unique finishes. Jon took $5,000 in savings and bought parts from overseas suppliers. He partnered with a local mechanic and started souping up cars with high-end finishes, audio systems, and engine work. The business took off and became one of the main suppliers for a popular TV show, making him millions by the time he was 16.

PLANNING MAKES PERFECT

MAYBE you're reading this and suddenly a thousand business ideas are bubbling through your brain. Or maybe you got distracted and are thinking about how many grilled cheese sandwiches it would take to fill up the Statue of Liberty. Either way, you need a plan—a **business plan**.

With a business plan, you can spot problems before you get started, problems that are way easier to fix now, with the "delete" key, rather than after you've invested your time and money. You wouldn't want to make 1,000 blue widgets before realizing that your customers only wanted red ones, would you?

Your business plan can be really simple to start. In fact, it can be just one page. We've provided a spectacular (if we do say so ourselves) *One-Page Business Plan* template on page 126. If you have an idea about how to start a business, this is a great way to figure out the details. If you don't have an idea, use it as a tool to inspire you. But before you skip right to it, consider these four steps:

STEP 1: "THE BIG IDEA?"

A strong, successful business starts with a great idea. If you already have an idea in mind, awesome. Write it down on your *One-Page Business Plan* where it says "The Big Idea?"

Drawing a blank? Relax—try this: Write down your answers to each prompt on the next page and you could turn those things into moneymakers! Need more inspiration? Search the Internet, ask friends and family—do anything you can to get ideas. But be realistic—don't count on inventing the next iPhone overnight.

THE FOUR Ds OF A GREAT BUSINESS IDEA

YOU have a few good ideas, but how do you choose? Use the Four Ds of a great business idea to help you decide. Drumroll, please . . .

How to Turn $100 into $1,000,000

- **DIFFERENT** You don't have to invent antigravity popcorn. You just have to come up with a way to make your popcorn stand out. Maybe use special herbs and spices or a cool container?

- **DESIRABLE** Your makeup videos might be mostly desired by preteens. They are your future customers (your "**target market**") so go out and find them!

Antigravity popcorn: the perfect weight-free snack

- **DYNAMIC** Your big idea doesn't have to be exciting to everyone, just your customers—and hopefully to you. It could be as simple as dog walking or as unique as handmade raincoats for Chihuahuas. A business will take up a big chunk of time. You might as well enjoy it.

THINK ABOUT...	EXAMPLE ANSWER	EXAMPLE MONEY-MAKING IDEA	YOUR ANSWER	POSSIBLE MONEY-MAKING IDEA
Something you enjoy	Riding my bike	Bike tours of my town/city		
Something you're really good at	Helping my parents with their computer	Computer services for the elderly		
Something you care about	The environment	Helping people find green products		
Something people need that they don't have now	A better backseat organizer for kids' stuff	Make one!		
Whom do you admire, and what does that person do?	My grandma, who bakes amazing pies	Sell pies based on her secret recipes		

- **DOABLE** Low-earth orbit tours might be too much too soon. Try something simpler.

STEP 2: MARKETING MADNESS

WHETHER you sell a product or a service, without **marketing**, you're just playing store. Marketing is how you get the word out about your new business. It can range from showing the product in person and putting out flyers, to having a website or pulling banners behind airplanes.

Before you can think about marketing to customers, identify who they are. Potential customers are known as your target market—the folks who might buy your product or service. Remember those handmade raincoats for Chihuahuas? No point targeting people who don't have a dog. Are those raincoats a luxury item? You might want to target people who have some extra cash to spare. So instead of posting flyers in apartment buildings that don't allow pets, you might want to put an ad in the community newsletter of an affluent dog-friendly neighborhood. Get the picture?

THE FOUR Ps OF MARKETING

ONCE you know your target market, there are four more things to consider, and you're in luck, these all start with *P*: product, price, place, and promotion.

1. PRODUCT

The actual thing you are selling your customers is your product. The decisions you need to consider in this category include things like: Do you have a logo or brand name? What sizes or features come with the product or service? What's the packaging? What kind of quality will you provide? Will you offer any money-back guarantees? When you think of "product," think of the whole enchilada—the entire value that you plan to offer your customers.

2. PRICE

What's the price of your product or service? There are a few good ways to figure out the right amount to charge:

EASY BUSINESS IDEAS FOR KIDS

SERVICES

- Take pictures or videos of pets, kids, or family events
- Wrap gifts or decorate houses for the holidays
- Teach or use computer skills for data entry, word processing, or for creating brochures, posters, and websites
- Teach music lessons or tutor students
- Babysit or be a parent helper
- Teach swimming lessons
- Pet-sit, wash dogs, or be a dog walker
- House-sit or take care of plants
- Offer house cleaning services such as vacuuming, washing floors and windows, or organizing garages, attics, and cabinets
- Wash cars and driveways
- Run errands. Grocery shop, then carry and put away food
- Paint or stain fences or furniture
- Mow lawns, rake leaves, or shovel snow
- Entertain: Be a clown, musician, or magician at kids' birthday parties
- Organize yard sales and other events for neighbors
- Collect and return bottles and cans

PRODUCTS

- Design and make products to sell:
  - baked goods, candy, pet treats
  - birdhouses and feeders
  - decorated T-shirts and sneakers
  - knitted hats, mittens, and scarves
  - picture frames
  - greeting cards
  - holiday decorations
  - jewelry
  - key chains
  - purses
  - soap and candles
  - starter plants for gardens
- Buy and sell used bikes and toys
- Create a stand to sell lemonade, juice, fruit and veggies, flowers, etc.
- Sell clothes at a consignment shop
- Sell used books, CDs, or DVDs to local stores or through a website
- Buy broken electronics, fix them, and sell them
- Buy food or candy items in bulk, then sell for a higher price
- Buy a vending machine
- Breed chickens, rabbits, or pigs and sell for a profit

PRODUCTS VS. SERVICES

Still not sure what business to start? No matter what business you choose, from a lemonade stand to computer repair, it will be a **product**, a **service**, or a combination of both.

SERVICES

Services are an easy way to get started. Think yard work, babysitting, cleaning, and so on. But you're limited by the number of hours you can work in a single day unless you hire employees.

PRODUCTS

Products are a little trickier to figure out. You'll need funding for supplies, and it can be challenging to find something unique to sell. If your products are popular, however, you can earn good money.

- Calculate your cost of making one unit and add a percentage for profit. Let's say you sell jam and it costs you $3.00 a jar to make. If you want to make at least a 25% profit, then you would add 25% of $3.00, which means you would price each jar at $3.75.

- Research competitors and charge just above or below their price.

- Ask people what they'd be willing to pay.

- Try selling your product or service at a certain price and adjust based on the results. Doing well? You might raise the price. Not selling? Lower it.

Remember, your price is also the value you give customers. If other neighborhood kids are mowing lawns, offer to mow lawns *and* weed flower beds for the same price. If you're selling cookies, put them in a cute container. These things make your product more valuable.

3. PLACE

Where can your customers obtain your product or service? Will it be online or in a brick-and-mortar store? Think about where you can find your target market, and make it convenient for them to get your stuff. If you're cleaning cars, you need to figure out where the people with dirty cars might be. Position your product where likely customers can easily get it when they want it most.

Ever notice how grocery stores put the nacho cheese dip right next to the tortilla chips? The store probably sells a lot more dip using this technique.

4. PROMOTION

Now it's time to get the word out. With your first business, you want maximum impact for minimum dollars. Here are nine strategies for catching customers' eyes and ears.

WORD OF MOUTH.

People believe other people more than they believe ads. Ask happy customers to tell their pals. Even better, offer a *discount* if they bring in a friend.

START A WEBSITE.

There are tons of free or low-cost website services, and, of course, blogs are always free. Don't get fancy—not at first. Just pick a basic template, write your pitch, and send the link to everyone you know.

SPONSOR AN EVENT.

Offer to help at a school, church, or community event. Ask if you can put up a poster or flyer about your product or service in exchange.

GET BUSINESS CARDS.

Even in today's high-tech world the good old paper-based traditional card is still needed.

SCORE FREE PRESS.

Write to local newspapers about your business and make sure to mention that you're a kid entrepreneur. You're a walking human-interest story.

Promote those puppy coats!

FUNDING FROM THE CROWD

Crowd funding is one way of raising the money you need to either launch or grow a business. It's the practice of soliciting monetary contributions from a large group of people, typically via websites. Usually, donors get something out of it, like a cool watch or a signed movie poster, and other times—just the good karma that they helped someone get a business off the ground.

MAKE FLYERS. Then print tons of copies and hang them on public bulletin boards.

WRITE AN ARTICLE. We're not talking the *New York Times* here. Small local publications often accept contributed content. Some bloggers do, too. Position yourself as knowledgeable—just make sure to include some contact information.

WEAR YOUR BRAND. Have a couple of T-shirts made up with your company logo on them. It will be a great conversation starter!

MAKE A VIDEO. Again—nothing fancy. Just a simple video (you can use your phone or borrow one) showcasing your product or expertise. Upload it so anyone can view it, and don't forget to send out the link!

STEP 3: CAN YOUR IDEA MAKE MONEY?

YOU'VE got a business idea, now it's time to follow the First Law of Business Success: Make a **profit**.

Profit is what's left over after all the bills are paid.

Your income must be higher than your expenses to have a profit. If you're providing a **service**, your income is what you charge per hour multiplied by the number of hours you expect to work. If you're providing a **product**, it's how many items you expect to sell multiplied by the price. Use a time frame over which to estimate your income, like a month or a year as a starting point.

Your expenses are the costs of running your business. Calculate everything you'll spend on your business in that month or year. Include the obvious stuff like the cost of supplies, as well as less obvious stuff like the cost of marketing materials.

For big purchases, you can spread the cost out over a longer time period. Just divide the total cost by the number of months you plan to pay off the expense, and include one month's worth of the expense in your estimate. Let's say you buy a $300 lawn mower for your yard care business and you're going to spread that over the first year of your business. You would divide $300 by 12 months, which equals $25 per month. So you include the $25 as a monthly expense, for 12 months.

Subtract total expenses from total income and you'll have an estimate of whether or not your business can make a profit. If you get a negative number and it doesn't look like you can make a profit, try adjusting things. Can you get materials cheaper? Can you charge a higher price? Can you reduce your marketing budget? Keep moving stuff around until you come out with a positive number. If it's still not working, try another idea or get some advice. That's the great thing about having a business plan before actually starting a business.

GET A SEPARATE ACCOUNT

IF you mix business money together with your personal money, it makes profitability much harder to track. You have already opened a personal savings account by now, so it should be pretty easy to set up a separate business account at the same bank or credit union. Just ask; they'll be happy to help. Also, keep receipts for *every* business expense. Yeah, we know, "Receipts! You mean that stuff I throw away?" Yes. This will help you add up what you're spending and save you a ton of money when filing your taxes—welcome to the real world of business!

TRACK IT OR LOSE IT

MONTHLY EXPENSES

Mower Payment to Bank of Dad	$50
Gas & Oil	$30
Blade Sharpening	$10
Fertilizer	$25
TOTAL EXPENSES	**$115**

MONTHLY INCOME

JOB TYPE	JOBS PER WEEK	HOURS PER JOB	HOURLY RATE	$$$ PER WEEK	$$$ PER MONTH
Basic Mow	4	1	$10	$40	$160
Mow & Trim	2	2	$10	$40	$160
Mow, Trim, Weed	1	3	$10	$30	$120

TOTAL MONTHLY INCOME	$440
SUBTRACT MONTHLY EXPENSES	$115
TOTAL MONTHLY PROFIT	$325

 Livi is doing pretty well. One thing she needs to consider, though, is that depending on where she lives, she might be able to run her business only in the spring and summer. She might need to invest in a rake and a snow shovel for the fall and winter.

Business is all about making a profit. Track your income and expenses in a separate budget to be sure your bank balance is headed in the right direction. You can use fancy software, or you can use a ratty spiral-bound notebook—both will do the job. Many people use online budget apps for tracking income and expenses. Just find the way that works for you.

Here are a couple of examples of budgets for small businesses.

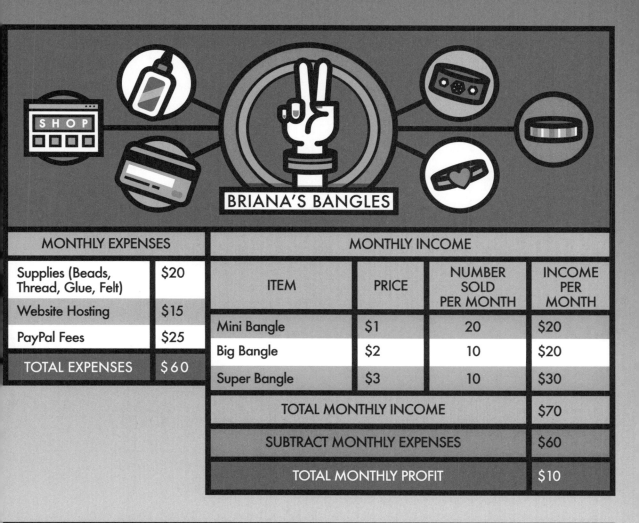

BRIANA'S BANGLES

MONTHLY EXPENSES	
Supplies (Beads, Thread, Glue, Felt)	$20
Website Hosting	$15
PayPal Fees	$25
TOTAL EXPENSES	$60

MONTHLY INCOME			
ITEM	PRICE	NUMBER SOLD PER MONTH	INCOME PER MONTH
Mini Bangle	$1	20	$20
Big Bangle	$2	10	$20
Super Bangle	$3	10	$30
TOTAL MONTHLY INCOME			$70
SUBTRACT MONTHLY EXPENSES			$60
TOTAL MONTHLY PROFIT			$10

 Briana's only making $10 a month in profit! She needs to step up her marketing, cut her costs, or improve her products to increase sales. Luckily, because she was tracking her income and expenses, she can fix things fast.

STEP 4: OPEN FOR BUSINESS

HAVE you nailed the details in your business plan? Good. Now it's time to stop planning and start doing. Make a batch of your product and test it on a friendly audience. Start offering services to neighbors whom you know. Hey, right now, competitors could be taking money that belongs to *you*! Are you going to let them do that? Get cracking!

WHAT IF THINGS GO GREAT?

YOU start your business, and everything goes according to plan. Nice work! Enjoy your success and start saving money to meet your long-term goal of making $1 million, but don't rest on your laurels.

- **ALWAYS BE ON THE LOOKOUT.** Are there ways to make your product or service better?

- **STAY AHEAD.** To keep up with the competition, do lots of research and talk to your customers to learn about the latest trends.

- **GET HELP.** Pick brains (not literally, of course). Ask friends and family members to pitch in, or even pay someone to help you if you're bringing in enough cash.

- **INVEST.** Put some of your profits toward marketing, better equipment, and training. It's one of the best ways to make your business (and money) grow.

WHAT IF THINGS GO NOT-SO-GREAT?

YOU start your business, and not quite everything goes according to plan. You're not making as much money as you hoped. Don't give up!

- **DON'T PANIC.** Keep marketing yourself—success may be closer than you think.

- **ADJUST.** Figure out what's wrong and try to fix it. Are your prices too high? Are you targeting the wrong customers?

How to Turn $100 into $1,000,000

- **ENJOY THE RIDE.** Hopefully, your business is based on something you like. Relax, have fun, and see if things pick up.

- **TRY AGAIN.** If your first business idea doesn't work, go back and try something else. The more swings you take, the more hits you'll have.

Don't scam Uncle Sam.

NO FUNNY BUSINESS

You may be a kid, but you still have to give Uncle Sam his cut (aka "taxes"). If you make more than a certain amount in a year you may have to pay self-employment taxes, unless you're doing household jobs like babysitting or lawn mowing and are under 18. Best to check with the **IRS**— The **Internal Revenue Service** (if you don't know what that is, you'll find out soon enough!).

The IRS offers free tax advice, so check its website, irs.gov. Tax laws change all the time, so keep track of what's required—you don't want the IRS coming back to grab your millions because you didn't pay your share in taxes. Happens to millionaires all the time. And if you really start raking in the dough, talk to an accountant. They're pretty good at this stuff.

SERIAL ENTREPRENEURS

A quick look at a few billionaires shows they are serial entrepreneurs, meaning they didn't stop at just one cool money-making idea—they kept going. From teaching disco lessons, to creating their own magazines, to orbiting the Earth, these billionaires have covered it all.

OPRAH WINFREY
MAXIMUM POWER!

- Gets first job at a corner grocery store.
- At 16, reads news on air at local radio station.
- At 19, is hired as a TV news co-anchor.
- Becomes anchor of *A.M. Chicago*, which is renamed *The Oprah Winfrey Show*.
- Forms her own production company, Harpo Productions, Inc.
- Produces the movie *Beloved*.
- Launches *O, The Oprah Magazine*, and the Oxygen Network, a 24-hour cable channel.
- Invests more than $1 million to bring the musical *The Color Purple* to Broadway.
- XM Satellite Radio begins broadcasting *Oprah and Friends*.
- Launches her own TV network, OWN.

MARK CUBAN
MAXIMUM POWER!

- At 12, sells garbage bags to pay for a pair of basketball shoes.
- As a college freshman, offers dance lessons to help pay for tuition.
- Gets a job at a bank.
- Starts selling PC software.
- Founds a software programming and consulting company.
- Starts his own Internet radio company, broadcast.com.
- Purchases the *Dallas Mavericks* for $285 million.
- Launches a group of media companies.
- Works with ABC to produce a reality-TV series.
- Invests in high-tech toilet seats.
- Joins as a cast member of the hit reality-TV series *Shark Tank*.

RICHARD BRANSON
MAXIMUM POWER!

- At 11, sells Christmas trees and birds to friends at school.
- Starts the magazine *Student* at 16.
- Founds *Virgin*, a mail-order record company.
- Opens a *Virgin* record store in London.
- Forms the *Virgin Records* music label.
- Launched *Virgin Books*.
- Starts *Virgin Atlantic* airlines.
- Creates *Virgin Mobile*.
- Creates *Virgin Money*.
- Invests in the renewable energy sector through Virgin Green Fund.
- Unveils a commercial spacecraft designed to send passengers into orbit for $200,000 a ticket.
- Opens first *Virgin Hotel*.

DON'T BE AFRAID TO FAIL

First business not working out? You're in good company. The difference between success and failure is often a willingness to stick to it. Colonel Sanders, founder of Kentucky Fried Chicken, tried to sell his chicken recipe to more than 1,000 restaurants before one decided to give his herbs and spices a shot. And remember our earlier examples of Thomas Edison and Steve Jobs? One thing they all had in common? A plan. If something isn't working, go back to the plan and figure out where things went wrong. Maybe you'll be the next Colonel Sanders!

LONG STORY SHORT

1. Have a plan. A solid business plan will increase your chances of success by allowing you to think through challenges before you get started. Remember the Four Ps and Four Ds.

2. Start small. You'll want to start your business without spending much money. Maybe that means just printing up flyers to pass around the neighborhood for your deck washing business.

3. Track your money. Open a separate bank account and keep track of your income and expenses. It's the only way to know if you're making a profit over time.

4. Get out there and do it. Even the best business idea is just an idea. Building a business takes hard work and perseverance—especially if it's going to help you save $1 million.

Chapter 7:
SAVE, SAVE, SAVE

EVERYBODY knows how to spend money. You hand over the cash and you get what you want. The problem is having money to hand over in the first place. If all you know how to do is spend money, you'll never become a millionaire.

However, if you save like a millionaire saves, you won't have to save like mad your whole life. You'll have to save up only a fraction of $1 million and let your money do the rest. And the faster you start learning to save, the sooner you'll get to your goal.

SAVING IS COOL

SOME people think saving money is uncool. They think if they *look* like a millionaire, they *are* one. But, sadly, they aren't and may never be. As you grow older, you'll hear story after story of someone who had a lot of money but didn't have the discipline to save it, or even worse: someone who went into thousands of dollars of debt.

Building up a chunk of change can be the *ultimate* cool. And the more you save, the more financial power and self-esteem you build. Train yourself to save. Think of saving money as a lifetime game. With a little practice, you can become quite good at it.

HOW TO SAVE MONEY
(THE SHORT VERSION)

Don't spend it. *The End*.
Seriously, don't spend it.
Thank you.

HOW TO SAVE MONEY
(THE LONG VERSION)

MAYBE saving money is a *little* bit more complicated than that. In theory, saving is easy: keep the money that is coming in (income) higher than the money going out (expenses). But how do you know when to save and when to spend? How do you keep all those sneaky temptations under control? And how do you protect your big, fat, ever-growing pile of money? The trick is knowing **needs** from **wants**.

GIMME WHAT I NEED, WHAT I REALLY, REALLY NEED

EVERY once in a while you'll hear about the student who lived on ramen noodles so he could save up enough money to start his own business. Most people are not born with that kind of self-control. That's where knowing wants from needs comes in.

Needs can be pretty basic: food, water, clothing, and shelter. Wants are things we desire—things we think will make us feel good or make life more convenient or make people notice us. We won't die without them—but we feel a strong desire to spend our money on them. You need water. You want designer fizzy water. You need shelter. You want a mansion. You need transportation. You want a sports car. If you can separate wants from needs, you will have a far easier time making decisions to help you save money. Ask yourself:

"If I don't get _____, will I actually, physically die?"

If the answer to the question is no, congratulations! You don't need that thing and you don't have to spend that money. Maybe we're being a little over the top, yet almost everybody wants more than they need. Limiting spending is a discipline you have to learn.

BANK ON IT

WHEN we talk about saving money we don't mean hiding some cash in the sock drawer. Why? Saving is hard if there's a big wad of cash burning a hole in your pocket, screaming "Spend me! Spend me!" in its wee little money voice. Avoid the temptation to spend and shut that money up in a **bank** or **credit union**. Why? Because once you spend your

TODAY'S MENU

—— **BREAKFAST** ——

ramen

—— **LUNCH** ——

ramen

—— **DINNER** ——

ramen

cash it's gone forever. Or you can lose it. Or a family member can "borrow" it and forget to return it! Or it can literally be stolen.

To safely and effectively save money, you have to open a savings account at a bank or credit union. Then start making regular deposits to that account. This is the best way to start saving toward that $1 million. We repeat:

THIS IS THE BEST WAY TO START SAVING TOWARD THAT $1 MILLION.

SAVE IT FOR LATER

There are three important reasons to put your money in a savings account at a bank or credit union:

1. **SAFETY.** Banks and credit unions keep your money safe. Safer than safe. Safer than your piggy bank kind-of-safe. It's protected by a government insurance plan. So even if the bank is robbed, your money will be safe and sound.

2. **INTEREST.** Banks will pay you for letting them use your money. Seriously. It's called "interest." We talked about this a little earlier. Both banks and credit unions loan the money you deposit (after holding on to a reserve) to other people or companies for a higher rate of interest. These days, they don't pay very much interest, but it's more than what your money is earning in your sock drawer.

3. **LESS TEMPTATION TO SPEND IT.** There's an old saying: "Out of sight, out of mind." If your money is locked away, you have less temptation to spend it. Having it in a financial institution adds a safeguard against sudden spur-of-the-moment decisions to blow some cash.

BANK OR CREDIT UNION?

BANKS and credit unions offer many of the same products or services, but there are some differences.

Banks are for-profit and earn money for shareholders (people who own stock in the bank). Banks offer a wide range of services from savings and checking accounts to a variety of investment options. Virtually all savings accounts at most banks are insured by the FDIC, or Federal Deposit Insurance Corporation, in case your money is lost or stolen.

Credit unions are not-for-profit and are owned by members (the customers of the credit union). Their main mission is to serve their members. That means they may sometimes pay more interest on savings accounts and charge lower fees than many banks. Anyone can become a member of a credit union, but some are available only to people living in the state where they are located. All credit unions have checking and savings accounts and some have a larger list of services, like small business and home loans. Your money is also insured, much like a bank, through the NCUA, or National Credit Union Administration.

If you want a fee-free ATM on every corner, a big national bank might be best for you. If you want higher interest and lower fees, consider a credit union. The important thing is to make the right choice for your financial goals.

SKIP THE SOCK DRAWER.

OPEN A SAVINGS ACCOUNT

ONE type of savings account is called a **custodial account**. If you're under 18 (or 21, depending on where you live) you'll need a parent or guardian to help you open this type of account. That grown-up is called the custodian, and just as the custodian at your school maintains the building, the custodian of your savings account maintains your money (only with less mopping). Make sure the custodian you pick is someone you really trust! Hopefully, that person will let you make as many decisions as possible about your money, so

If you stack up a million one-dollar bills, it would be 350 feet tall (that's 107 meters for readers in most of the world). Start stacking your money in a savings account today!

it's really like the savings account belongs to you. It will when you turn 18 (or 21, again, depending on the state where you live).

Here are some other important things to know about custodial accounts:

• The money in a custodial account belongs to you by law. However, the custodian is the only one who can perform transactions.

• Many custodial accounts will let the account owner (that's you!) check your balance online just like with a regular account.

350

IN-SCHOOL CREDIT UNIONS

Did you know there are more than 900 in-school credit unions around the country? That's a credit union right inside your school for students, run by students. Talk about easy access to lunch money! Most offer just savings and checking accounts, but if you're lucky enough to be a member of one of these, then you might not need a custodian on the account.

• A custodial savings account is designed for saving money. You can withdraw only a certain number of times per month or you get dinged with a fee.

The important thing is to open an account now! It might be the credit union around the corner (because you don't drive), or the bank with the most ATMs, or you can take the easy route and just use the same financial institution as your parents. Can you say "Direct deposit my allowance, please!"?

PAY YOURSELF FIRST

WE know we talked about this earlier, but it is so important we need to bring it up again. Hmm, what to do with your allowance? There's that new game to download, those new jeans, and you really "need" a new phone. How can you ever save anything if you're always paying for stuff?

The answer is, you don't—you Pay Yourself First (or PYF for short), every time.

PYF means every time money lands in your pocket or piggy bank, you put some of it away in your savings

Pay yourself first: It's the easiest trick in the book. Don't forget it! Write it down! Type it up! Write it in needlework!

account before you spend any of it. Basically, you make your savings goal *numero uno* before you start spending. It can be a certain dollar amount like $10 per paycheck or a percentage, say, 20% of your allowance. It should be included in your budget and be paid *first*. That's part of the PYF strategy: You make sure the money intended for your savings account hits the bank before you hit the stores!

And what's the easiest way to do the easiest trick in this book? Make it automatic. That means set up an automatic transfer every month from one account into a separate savings account. You can set this up through your bank or credit union. Maybe every month you transfer your monthly savings goal into a separate account, as an easy way to reach your goal (then you won't be tempted to spend it). Just remember to have enough money in your first account to do the transfer!

SAVING NOW = POWER LATER

BE consistent. It is crucial that you make regular deposits to your savings accounts, no matter how small, weekly or monthly. Keep it up. You might go three months or even six before you start noticing that you've "got money in the bank." But pretty soon, saving will become a habit. You just won't feel right until you've put a little bit of money away each week.

Your million dollar money plant might look small at first but keep saving and see what happens.

QUESTIONS TO ASK WHEN CHOOSING A BANK OR CREDIT UNION

Go visit several financial institutions and compare interest rates, fees, services, and incentives. Then pick the one that's best for you. There could be some conditions in the fine print, so remember to ask these questions:

• What interest rates do you pay on savings accounts? (It's going to be low, but that's okay for now.)

• What fees do you charge on savings or checking accounts?

• How much do you charge if I overdraw my account? ("Insufficient Funds" fees can be charged to you if you spend more than what's in your account. These can really hurt. Like hundreds of dollars' worth of hurt. So, think like a millionaire and always keep a minimum balance in your account.)

• What's the minimum amount I need to open a savings account?

• How many branch locations do you have?

• Where are your ATMs located?

• Do you offer online banking? (C'mon, it's the 21st century! If they don't offer it, get outta there!)

• Do you have any mobile apps?

Even with small amounts, if you make saving a habit, over time that balance will grow, and grow, and grow! To get you started, here are some savings tricks of the rich and famous (and not-so-famous):

- Save unexpected windfalls. Put that twenty bucks your uncle sent you right in the bank.

- Avoid impulse buys.

- Track your spending in a budget.

- Always be thinking of ways to cut your expenses.

- Leave debit cards and credit cards (if you're old enough to have them) at home—use cash instead. You'll spend less.

- Never pay full price—use the Internet to research the best deals.

- Bring lunch to school instead of spending money.

- Shop around for financial institutions with the best interest rates.

- Make savings automatic—set up automatic transfers to a savings account.

- Find ways to make saving money a game. How much can you sock away this month? You can even make it a competition between friends—a race to a million dollars!

THE BEST THINGS IN LIFE ARE FREE!

Becoming a millionaire means *not* spending your money. Does that mean *not* having fun? Far from it. Just go online and search for free activities in your city. You'll find tons of ways to kill some time without killing your wallet. Here are some ideas:

- Most museums have a free day during the month.

- Nature is almost always free. Get something to throw or kick and head for the park.

- See what's new at the library. Check out the latest issues of all the financial publications, check out movies, too! And these things called books! All free!

- Create a "Cheap Club" with friends. The club meets once a month and the hosts are tasked with coming up with food and entertainment on a very stingy budget, like $5 per person.

FLEX THOSE SAVINGS MUSCLES

Just like a bodybuilder makes a habit of lifting weights, to reach your savings goal, you'll need to make a habit of saving money. So get creative, get disciplined, and pump some muscle into your savings account. If you make a few mistakes along the way, no worries. A few sacrifices here and there will get you back on track.

($0.56 closer to your $500 goal and eventually, $1 million!)

More interest earned!

SHORT-TERM GOAL= Save **$500** in **one year**

Open savings account and make first deposit. Yay!

Leave debit card at home and use cash only.

Go to mall with friends and blow budget. :(

($1.73 Hey, every little bit helps!)

Earn interest.

Pay Yourself First. Make deposits into savings account every Friday.

(−$37.52)

FREE DAY! Play frisbee with friends instead of going to the mall.

Start spending diary. :)

($11 added)

Deposit extra money into account.

(No matter how small!)

Buy used books for school.

(save $78)

BACK ON TRACK!

Get MDM back! Sell old clothes online to make up for budget blunder.

(save $21)

Postpone going to movies next month.

Bring lunch to school.

(save $5)

(save $5)

($27 back in my pocket)

Money is tight this month. Take extra babysitting job.

(save $6.41)

Research best online deals for makeup.

Deposit entire allowance this month!

Bring lunch to school.

($45)

(Woo-hoo! $50 added)

START TODAY!

OK, maybe we're beginning to sound like a broken **record** (for those of you who don't know what a record is, check the glossary), but none of the information in this book will matter if you don't think like a millionaire and start saving today.

Can you condition your mind and discipline yourself to control your spending? Can you pay yourself first on a regular basis? Can you be patient and keep saving? Yes? Good, because, at first, the amounts you're saving may seem teeny and insignificant. Then one day you'll wake up and notice you have a thousand bucks in your savings account. Stand by because we're about to share the not-so-secret secret to launch you on your way to being a real millionaire!

LONG STORY SHORT

1. Think about not spending money.

2. Know the difference between wants and needs.

3. Open a savings account and make regular deposits, and save, save, save!

4. Pay yourself first (PYF).

5. Did we mention save, save, save?

Chapter 8:
THE POWER OF COMPOUND INTEREST

EINSTEIN never said "compound interest is the most powerful force in the universe." But if he had, he'd be right. **Compound interest** is the most powerful force in the universe. Okay, the point can be argued, but in the case of this book, compound interest is, dare we say it, *The Most Powerful Force in the Universe* if you are going to grow your money from $100 to $1 million.

Got your attention? Thought so.

QUESTION:

Which would you rather have?

A. $1 million

B. One penny, doubled every day, for a month. (One penny the first day, then two pennies the next, then four pennies the third day, then eight pennies on the fourth day, and so on, and so on. . . .)

C'mon, you know this is a setup. Do the math!

HINT: The answer has something to do with the power of compounding.

Okay, for the lazy:
Answer: A isn't bad, but you want to pick Answer: B. One penny, doubled every day for a month, is $5,368,709.12! Holy Compound Interest, Mr. Lincoln!

STAND BY FOR THE SECRET

WHEN you put your money in a savings account, in a way you're lending money to the bank. Remember when we told you the bank pays you a little something called interest to encourage you to keep your money there (instead of buying a hundred pounds of Red Vines)? Good.

Imagine that you have $100 in a savings account earning **simple interest**. That interest is based on the **principal** (the money you have in the account), in this case $100. Let's say your $100 is earning 5% interest per year, and you're not adding any more money to the

THE S

STARTS R

account. That means you would earn $5 the first year, $5 the second year, and so on. After 10 years you'll have $150 in your account.

HERE COMES MIND BLOWING!

WITH compound interest you earn *interest on your interest*. Yes, it's true! Now imagine that you have $100 principal in an account earning compound interest at the same 5% per year. You would still earn $5 the first year, for a total of $105, but by the second year, things would start to get interesting. The compound interest paid is based on the principal ($100)

COMPOUND INTEREST FORMULA

Here is the official mathematical formula for compound interest. Go ahead, Einstein, figure it out:

$$A = P \left(1 + \frac{R}{N}\right)^{NT}$$

where:

A = amount accumulated

P = principal amount (initial investment)

R = annual nominal interest rate (not reflecting the compounding)

N = number of times the interest is compounded per year

NT = number of years the money is borrowed for

THE RULE OF 72

Want a quick way to determine how many years it will take to double your money? Just divide 72 by the fixed annual interest rate. It's not perfectly accurate, but it will put you in the ballpark for interest rates less than 20%. For example, if you invest $100 at 10% per year, you would divide 72 by 10: 72/10 = 7.2 years.

So it will take approximately 7.2 years to double your money, if you can earn an average of 10% interest per year—challenging but not impossible.

MONEY MOMENT

Compound interest can also be used against you. When it comes to credit cards and compound interest, time is not on your side. Credit card companies are using compound interest to calculate what you owe. And it's high—usually somewhere from 12% to 30%! The longer you have the debt, the more the interest grows.

plus the $5 interest from that first year. So you're actually being paid 5% on $105. That would be $110.25. In the third year, compound interest would be paid on the original $100 plus two years' worth of interest, or $115.51. In 10 years, instead of having just $150 to show for your saving efforts, you'd have $162.89. That is almost 9% more money over the same time period because you earned interest on your interest.

WHAT THIS MEANS TO YOU

This means that if you want to eventually have $1 million, you don't actually have to save up one million $1 bills. You need to save up only enough money so that, over time, your money begins to work for you, earning compounding interest.

WHAT'S THE CATCH?

COMPOUND interest isn't magic—it's just math. As your amount of principal and interest builds up, your total amount of money starts to grow faster and faster and faster.

(Continued on page 89)

TIME REALLY IS MONEY

The earlier you let that compound interest train get rollin', the faster and bigger you can build your money. Going back to the example of $100 in savings, let's imagine you left that money in a savings account at 5% and just ignored it. With simple interest, in 50 years, you'd have $350. That's pretty good, considering you didn't have to lift a finger. But with compound interest, you'd have a whopping $1,146.74! All from your original hundred bucks! Look what happens when your original investment of $100 is actually $1,000 and we change the interest rate to 10%.

COMPOUND INTEREST 10% for 50 YEARS

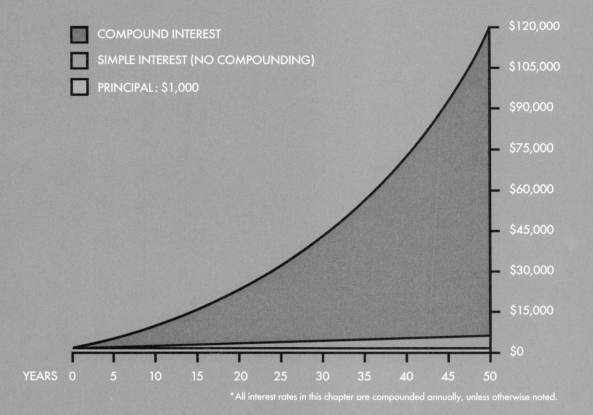

COMPOUND INTEREST

SIMPLE INTEREST (NO COMPOUNDING)

PRINCIPAL : $1,000

$120,000

$105,000

$90,000

$75,000

$60,000

$45,000

$30,000

$15,000

$0

YEARS 0   5   10   15   20   25   30   35   40   45   50

*All interest rates in this chapter are compounded annually, unless otherwise noted.

THE SECRET WITHIN THE SECRET

Keep adding money to the principal on a regular basis. Then, using the power of compounding interest, things skyrocket! Take a look at both these examples:

Jamie and Erren, both 15 years old, each start with an initial investment of $5,000 saved up from their jobs, allowances, a birthday gift from Uncle Joe, and odd jobs for neighbors. Both save for 50 years and are able to earn an average of 8% return on their money. Jamie doesn't make any more contributions after her initial $5,000, but Erren continues to make yearly contributions of $1,000 to her account (that's $83.33 per month, which is doable for most adults).

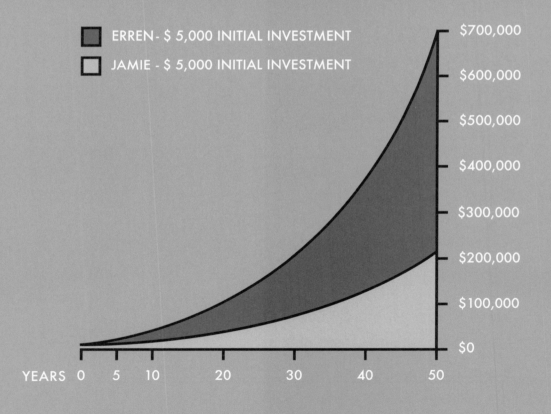

ERREN - $ 5,000 INITIAL INVESTMENT
JAMIE - $ 5,000 INITIAL INVESTMENT

$700,000
$600,000
$500,000
$400,000
$300,000
$200,000
$100,000
$0

YEARS 0   5   10   20   30   40   50

Wow! Look at the difference adding money to the principal made over the long term. Erren was able to grow her money exponentially, just by saving an extra $83.33 per month for 50 years. In just a few more years, she will reach $1 million. Impressive, huh?

Jackson and Layla want to become millionaires. Jackson started saving $1,000 per year at 15 years old. He was able to earn an average of 8% interest on his investments. Layla didn't start saving until she was 30 years old. Because Jackson was able to take advantage of the power of compound interest over a longer period of time, he was able to get to $1 million with less money—$85,000 *less* to be exact. Where Jackson invested $55,000 over the long term, Layla had to invest $140,000 to reach the same amount because she waited. Start saving as much as you can, as young as you can, to take full advantage of the power of compound interest.

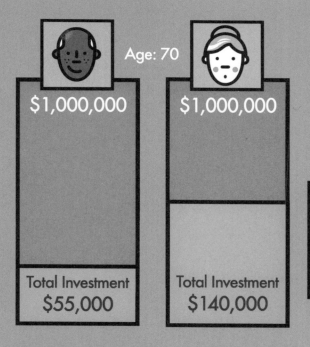

Age: 70

JACKSON INVESTS $1,000 PER YEAR FOR 55 YEARS

$1,000,000

$1,000,000

Total Investment $55,000

Total Investment $140,000

Jackson started saving when he was 15.

LAYLA INVESTS $3,500 PER YEAR FOR 40 YEARS

Layla didn't start saving until she was 30.

Both reach $1,000,000 by age 70 but Layla's total investment was $140,000. And Jackson only had to invest $55,000.

You will eventually have to move money into other accounts and investments that will compound at a higher interest rate. This will become your **"portfolio,"** which is just a fancy way of saying your "collection" of investments. We explain them more in the next chapter, but here's an example of compound interest at work when various investments are in the picture:

Georgia saves up $55,000 by the time she's 40. Look at the huge difference earning a higher percent of interest makes on her investment over the next 35 years.

If she left her $55,000 in a CD that earned 3% interest, after 35 years it would be $154,762.43. If instead she invested her $55,000 in bonds that returned on average 6% interest, then she would have $422,734.77. Wow! But take a look at what would happen if she invested her money in the stock market and was able to get a 9% return on her money—her investment almost triples to $1,122,768.24. Turns out Georgia is a really smart investor and was able to get an average of 12% return on her stock picks, and her mere $55,000 turns into a whopping $2,903,979.08, all due to the power of compound interest.

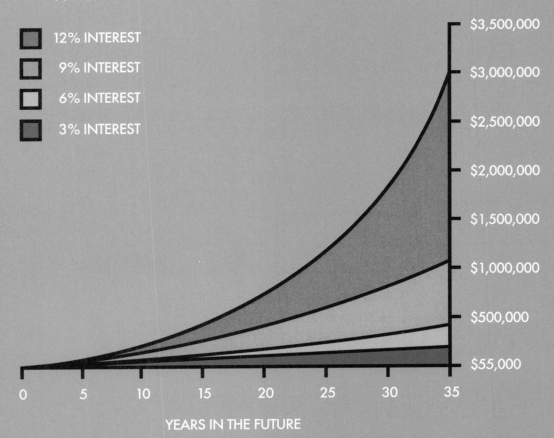

12% INTEREST
9% INTEREST
6% INTEREST
3% INTEREST

$3,500,000
$3,000,000
$2,500,000
$2,000,000
$1,500,000
$1,000,000
$500,000
$55,000

0   5   10   15   20   25   30   35

YEARS IN THE FUTURE

(Continued from page 84)

But don't stop adding money to the account—or worse, take any money out—or you'll lose the power of compounding. Keep adding money to the account or investment on a regular basis. Over time, your money will grow bigger, faster. Bottom line: When it comes to saving up a million dollars, you want to keep the pedal to the metal. Take a look at how much you'd have to save each month (approximately) to get $1 million, depending on how soon you want to reach your goal (assuming annual interest at 8% compounded monthly*).

> *Reach $1 million in 30 years = must save $706 a month*
> *TOTAL INVESTMENT = $254,160*

> *Reach $1 million in 40 years = must save $309 a month*
> *TOTAL INVESTMENT = $148,320*

> *Reach $1 million in 50 years = must save $140 a month*
> *TOTAL INVESTMENT = $84,000.*

* Taxes and inflation have not been factored into results.

NOW YOU KNOW THE SECRET

COMPOUNDING interest is the secret to saving up $1 million. It may involve a little math, but you don't need to be good with numbers to make $1 million, just good at saving money.

And it doesn't take an Einstein (like that segue?) to understand why it's important to start saving as young as you can. If compound interest is not the most powerful force in the entire universe, it is at least in the financial universe.

LONG STORY SHORT

• •

With compound interest, your money makes money and the money your money makes makes more money.

Chapter 9:
INVESTING

BY now you have hopefully achieved your short-term goal of saving up $100. Maybe you've been so inspired from reading this book that you've saved up $10,000! Congratulations!

A savings account is a great place to stash your money at first. It's safe and it pays you a little interest. But it won't make you $1 million—not in your lifetime anyway.

Getting to $1 million requires moving some of your money into investments with a higher **rate of return**. How

WHO IS WARREN BUFFETT?

Widely regarded as one of the most successful investors in history, Warren Buffett is also ranked as one of the richest men in the world, with a net worth of over $70 billion. Buffett is a famous investor because he takes a long-term approach and invests in companies with good business fundamentals that may be overlooked by others. He is the primary shareholder, chairman, and CEO of Berkshire Hathaway in Omaha, Nebraska, and lives in the same home he bought in 1958. Talk about having a Million-Dollar Mind-Set! Referred to as the "Sage" or "Oracle of Omaha," among investment professionals and the investing public, there is no more respected voice.

much more? Many financial advisers suggest your money should be growing, on average, somewhere between 5% and 12% per year. You'll never get that from a savings account.

Just compare $100 in a savings account earning 1% per year, with an investment earning 5% per year, and another earning 10% per year.

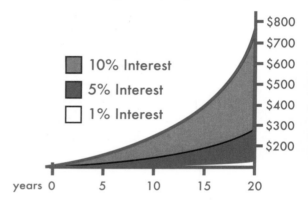

With 1% interest, you're earning just a few pennies per year. After 20 years you've made only $20. With 5% return, you more than double your money to $271.85. And with 10%? Your money multiplies over *seven times* to a whopping $738.70!

Of course, it's not quite that simple. You have to work for high investment returns. More important, investments aren't insured like your savings account. You take the risk of losing everything if your investment becomes less valuable. Smart investors should only invest money they're willing to lose.

WHAT IS INVESTING?

INVESTING means putting your money into something that can potentially make you *more* money. And the number of places where you can invest your money is staggering.

You can invest in just about anything. Anything! Enjoy skateboarding? You can invest in a company that makes skateboards or skateboard shoes. You can also invest in the company that makes the concrete in the skateboard park. You can even invest in the company that makes the fuel for the ambulance that carries your friend to the hospital after that missed plasma spin.

Whatever you invest in, you want it to be something that will become more valuable over time so your investment grows. Hopefully, as skateboarding becomes more popular, more skateboards are sold, and your investment in the skateboard company eventually becomes more valuable.

RISK AND REWARD

LIKE skateboarding, investing means taking a risk in the hope of a reward. In skateboarding, when you learn a new trick, you risk kissing the pavement for the reward of becoming a better skater. When you invest your money, you take the risk of kissing your money good-bye for the reward of possibly making more money. Are you willing to take that risk?

WHEN SHOULD YOU START?

YOU should build up a good chunk of savings first, and then invest only money that you're willing to risk losing. Don't risk what you've put aside for college tuition. Start slow.

Ask yourself, "Self, how much money am I comfortable with risking?"

(Continued on page 96)

You can invest in just about anything, and we mean anything—just make sure it increases in value over time.

THINGS PEOPLE INVEST IN

You can invest in almost anything. Here are some common investments that range in risk:

CDs, OR CERTIFICATES OF DEPOSIT

These are a great place to start because they're available at the bank or credit union where you already have your savings account. They're also low risk. CDs pay a little more interest than a common savings account, but you must leave your money invested for a set length of time to get the maximum return—usually a few weeks, to months, to years. While CDs generally don't compound at a high enough percentage rate to really make your savings take off, they are a great way to lock up your money so you don't spend it before you move it to another investment.

STOCKS

You become part owner of a **public company** that offers goods or services when you buy **shares** (aka "stock") in that company. You can invest in anything from "penny" stocks (high risk) to blue chip stocks (lower risk).

BONDS

You loan money to a company, or the government, with a promise that it will be repaid with interest. Bonds are rated by credit agencies according to how risky they are from AAA (low risk) to NR (not rated or high risk).

REAL ESTATE

You can invest directly in residential property (like your parents' home) or commercial property (like a shopping mall). Or you can invest indirectly through real estate investment trusts (REITs), which are traded as a stock on the various stock exchanges.

COMMODITIES

Commodities are raw materials that are used to make other things: precious metals (gold, silver, copper, etc.), coffee beans, lumber, oil—even pork bellies! Investors don't usually buy and sell commodities themselves but purchase a contract to buy them at a certain price.

COMPANIES

You can invest in a company directly by lending the owners money or becoming one of the owners yourself. This is risky, but it can also produce high returns.

ART AND ANTIQUES

The right piece of art can appreciate faster than almost any investment on the planet. But it has to be the right piece of art, and there are plenty that are not.

(Continued from page 93)

(Hint: All of it? No. Some of it? Yes.) Then start by placing a *small* portion of your savings into an investment you think will make money. This is the beginning of what is known as your investment portfolio, which is usually made up of a combination of different types of investments (see pages 94–95). Choose wisely and see if your investment goes up in value. If so, great! If not, don't panic. Ask why: Did you make the right investment? Maybe it just needs a little more time.

You will make some mistakes with your investments, especially at first. Don't be discouraged. Even the most experienced investors lose money. The key is to make more money than you lose. You increase your chances of doing that by taking your time and doing your research.

STOCK BASICS 101

YOU can invest in a lot of different things, but many people start with stocks. They're easy to buy, sell, and understand. They also historically outperform other investment options over the long-term.

A public company can raise money by selling portions of ownership called shares to the public through a **stock market**. (Privately held companies don't sell stock to the general public.) Buying a share of stock makes you a "shareholder," and you become a partial owner of that company. The company gets money to grow and you get to own a piece of a company. From railroads to space travel, shoelaces to software, the list of public companies that issue stock is huge!

Stocks are bought and sold. One person is buying a stock that they think will go up in value, while another person is selling that stock because they think it will go down (or they need money).

Stock prices represent the battle between those two thoughts. Who's right? Who knows? Multiply this by millions of shares of stock being bought and sold by millions of people every day, and you have a stock market.

BUY IT!

YOU can't buy stock like you go to the store to buy a bag of chips. Only specially licensed people called **brokers** can trade stocks. When you're ready to buy or sell a stock, you place an order and the broker executes it for you. Trading stocks isn't free—the brokerage usually charges a **commission** for this service, but it's worth it if you can make big profits. You may also want to take a look at online trading websites and apps—there are many to choose from, so do your research and pick the one that's best for you.

CHOOSING A BROKERAGE

YOU can get brokers working for you by opening a **brokerage account**. You can't have your own brokerage account until you reach 18 or older. But you can have your guardians open one for you, which (as with your savings account) is called a custodial account. You legally own the money in the account, but the custodian has to actually make the trades.

There are lots of brokerages out there, and you need to find one that's right for you. Here are three important things to keep in mind:

1. Your money is not insured like it is with a savings account. Choose a well-established company you can trust.

2. Trading stocks costs money, so try to choose a brokerage with low fees. The less you pay, the more you keep!

3. Choose a brokerage that lets you purchase partial shares (also called fractional shares). That means you can buy as much or as little of a stock as

(Continued on page 99)

BULL VS. BEAR

What is the long-term performance history of the stock market? Throughout stock market history, the average yearly return for periods of 25 years or longer has been around 9% to 10%. When stock prices are rising the market is said to be a **bull market**, and when it's on a downward trend it's said to be a **bear market**. The terms *bear* and *bull* are thought to derive from the way in which each animal attacks its opponents. That is, a bull will thrust its horns up into the air, whereas a bear will swipe down.

ALPHABET SOUP

If you listen to the news, you might hear what sounds like a bowl of alphabet soup: **NYSE, NASDAQ, DOW**. Listen up, because they're talking about the financial markets. Stocks and many other types of investments are bought and sold on an **exchange**. If a stock is available on an exchange, it's said to be **listed** there.

The two most popular and largest exchanges in the world are:

• **THE NEW YORK STOCK EXCHANGE** (usually printed as **NYSE**, but don't ever pronounce it as "nice-ee")

• **THE NATIONAL ASSOCIATION OF SECURITIES DEALERS AUTOMATED QUOTATIONS** (always called the **NASDAQ**, pronounced "nazz-dak")

What about those other letters you often hear? Like S&P 500 and the Dow? They are referring to an **index**. An index is like an imaginary grouping of stocks and can be a good indicator as to whether the market as a whole is going up or down. Two well-known indices are:

• **S&P 500**: "S&P" stands for **STANDARD AND POOR'S**, which is a **rating agency**. It recommends which stocks to buy and sell and also keeps track of the S&P 500. True to its name, it's based on 500 stocks and is the most commonly used benchmark for the health of the stock market.

• **DOW**: when people say "the Dow" they mean the **DOW JONES INDUSTRIAL AVERAGE**. It's similar to the S&P, except it tracks 30 really big companies. To be included in this index, a stock must be a leader in its industry and widely held by investors.

Watch these indices and get a sense for where the stock market is going overall. It pays to keep an eye on the general state of the market.

you want—even less than one share. With some stocks trading at hundreds of dollars a share, that can be a good thing!

CHOOSING YOUR FIRST STOCK

THERE are literally thousands of stocks to choose from. How do you go about picking your first one? If you want to invest in individual stocks, a good way to start is with companies you know. What is your favorite beverage? What shoes are you wearing? What snacks do you eat? Any of those businesses could be listed on a stock **exchange**. All you have to do is find the company's stock exchange symbol, and do some research. (*Never buy a stock without doing your research.*) You might also look at the top ten performing companies over the past few months or years. Pay particular attention to ones that have weathered **economic downturns**.

Your goal is to find good companies that will go up in value—not the one making the coolest thing. A great company doesn't equal a great investment. That's where doing your research as a young investor comes into play.

DO YOUR RESEARCH

There's a lot to research about each stock. The more experienced investor will want to know details like **P/E ratios**, 52-week high and low, and **market capitalization**, but here are some important basics to consider:

Profitability: Is the company making a profit? If not, will it be able to soon?

Growth prospects: Is the company expanding into new markets or hiring more employees?

Management: Do the key executives (aka bosses) have the experience to reach the company's goals?

Competitive Advantage: Does the company have a special or unique advantage compared to its competitors?

Finally, always remember that past performance is not a guarantee of future results.

PROTIP: There are tons of stock investing games with imaginary money. Try them out and avoid a bunch of rookie mistakes before risking your real cash in the stock market.

HOW DO YOU ACTUALLY MAKE MONEY?

BOUGHT your first stock? Congrats! Time is on your side, so hold on to your stock while it hopefully goes up in value. The key to profiting from an individual stock is to **buy low and sell high**. If the stock costs $10 and it goes up $2 over the course of a year, your investment has risen 20%. That's if you were to sell it. If you hold on to it, it may keep rising and may go up another $2 the next year. When you decide to sell your stock, the number of shares times the price you sell them for (minus the brokerage fees) gets deposited into your brokerage account.

Finding **undervalued** stocks and waiting until everyone else catches on is called **value investing**. It is a very popular investing style. It involves researching companies to understand their strengths and any risks they have, and then deciding if the stock price is fair. In many cases, strong but boring companies do not get as much attention from investors. A value investor would see this, buy the stock, and wait for its value to go up.

STOCK SPLITS

OCCASIONALLY, a company will authorize a splitting of the stock. It will do this to keep the price attractive to new investors and to reward current ones. It can vary, but many stocks will split 2 for 1. That means for every share you own, you now own two at half the original share price. Hopefully, the stock will rise back to the original price, and you can potentially double your money.

DELIGHTFUL DIVIDENDS

SOME companies pay a **dividend** on their stock. Dividends are a share of the company's profits that the company gives back to investors.

Dividend payments are usually made once every three months. They can often be fairly substantial—several percentage points of a stock's price (much more than you'd earn with a savings account). Dividends are paid per share, so the more shares you own, the more you collect. One more thing: Some financial analysts think dividend-paying stocks tend to do better over the long term. So a company with stock that pays dividends may be worth an extra look.

DON'T BE SHY— DIVERSIFY!

E VER heard the saying "Don't put all your eggs in one basket"? You don't want to own just one investment. You want to diversify. **Diversification** just means owning a bunch of different

SILLY SYMBOLS

Every company on a stock exchange is represented by a symbol. It's usually a few letters representing the company's full name, but some companies get clever.

STEINWAY (LVB): Piano maker honors famous pianist Ludwig van Beethoven

OLYMPIC STEEL (ZEUS): Steel manufacturer pays homage to a Greek god

MARKET VECTORS AGRIBUSINESS ETF (MOO): Must be in the cow business

HARLEY DAVIDSON (HOG): Motorcycle company plays up its famous nickname

ASIA TIGER FUND (GRR): Investment fund that sounds like an angry tiger

DYNAMIC MATERIALS (BOOM): Hmm . . . wonder if dynamite is involved?

NATIONAL BEVERAGE (FIZZ): Playful and catchy symbol for a beverage company

When you're young, you have time for your money to grow, and can take more risks and make mistakes, but when you get older you'll need to protect yourself.

stocks in different industries, and often mixing in other investment types as well. Why is diversification important? Because it spreads out your risk. The price of a single stock can change a lot from day to day. But when you add a whole bunch of stocks together, those swings are usually not as wild—and if they are, the entire market is doing it, too.

FUN WITH FUNDS

A GREAT way to diversify is to invest in multiple stocks at once using **mutual funds** and **index funds.**

- A mutual fund is an investment that packages together many types of investments. Some might hold only stocks; others might add bonds, real estate, or precious metals and other commodities to the mix.

- An index fund follows the total performance of a group of stocks. For example, SPY is the symbol for an index fund that follows the S&P 500.

Both kinds of funds can have a very broad range of stocks, or a very narrow one. There are funds that focus on technology, on socially responsible companies, or even ones that are just made up of stocks that pay dividends.

Some funds are run by people who do a lot of the research for you. You often pay a hefty fee for their expertise in the form of a "management fee." One thing to remember is that a fund can be great for the past five years and tank the next. Sometimes smart fund managers just turn out to be lucky ones—and luck can turn.

Other funds—especially index funds—are controlled by committees and/or algorithms, which are rules that automatically determine which stocks or bonds will be in the fund. Because there's no brainiac managing them, index funds often charge lower management fees.

Before you invest in a fund, read the details of the investment offering (called a **prospectus**). Be careful; some funds charge little or nothing making them a great deal for the beginning investor (assuming they go up!). Others charge hefty fees that can take a serious bite out of your profits.

The great thing about mutual funds and index funds is that they let you "own" a whole bunch of different stocks with every share you buy. That means you achieve instant diversification.

KNOW WHEN TO HOLD 'EM, KNOW WHEN TO FOLD 'EM

TIME is on your side. If you buy a stock and it goes down, you don't have to sell it right away. The same is true if the stock goes up. If you did your research and it's a solid company, you could try holding on to it and seeing where it goes. Stocks go up and down all the time—you don't earn or lose money until you sell the stock or the company goes out of business (yes, it happens). If it is a good quality stock, investors who hold over the long term are more likely to win out in the end.

WHERE TO RESEARCH

- **STOCK WEBSITES:** Big stock market websites have news, analyst reports, and historical charts for just about every stock across all the big exchanges. Some examples include: Investopedia, Motley Fool, Yahoo! Finance, The Street, and MSN Money.

- **FINANCIAL PAPERS:** Even if you don't understand all of what they say, financial newspapers like the *Wall Street Journal* or *Barron's* are great ways to learn and figure out what you might want to invest in.

- **COMPANY QUARTERLY EARNING REPORTS:** All publicly listed companies file a report on their earnings and losses at the end of each quarter. Read them before you invest.

- **YOUR BROKERAGE:** Once you have a brokerage account, you'll have access to tons of information about every stock under the sun.

- **FRIENDS AND FAMILY:** Ask people you know if they invest, what they invest in, and why.

ADVENTURES IN INVESTING

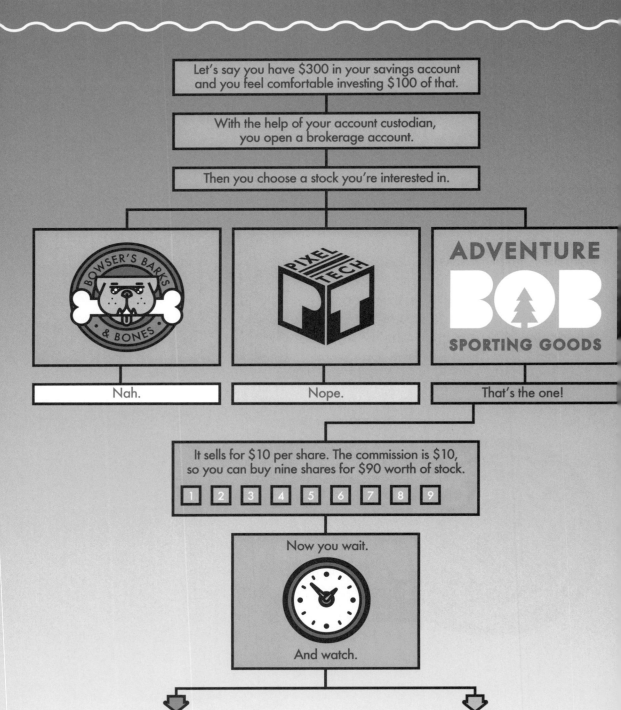

Let's say you have $300 in your savings account and you feel comfortable investing $100 of that.

With the help of your account custodian, you open a brokerage account.

Then you choose a stock you're interested in.

BOWSER'S BARKS & BONES

Nah.

PIXEL TECH

Nope.

ADVENTURE **BOB** SPORTING GOODS

That's the one!

It sells for $10 per share. The commission is $10, so you can buy nine shares for $90 worth of stock.

1 2 3 4 5 6 7 8 9

Now you wait.

And watch.

If the stock goes up, decide whether to keep it and hope it goes up more, or sell it and TAKE A PROFIT.

If the stock goes down, decide whether to hold on to it and hope it changes direction, or give up, sell it and TAKE A LOSS.

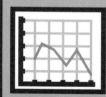 

Let's assume you made a good pick—the stock goes up 10% after a year! 10% of $90 is $9. Now you have $99 worth of stock.

What are your options?

SELL
You decide to sell the stock. But you forgot about that pesky commission! $99 minus $10 is $89. You started with $100, and your stock went up, but you still lost $11.

HOLD
You hold on to the stock for another year. The company does great, and your stock grows another 10%. Now your stock is worth $108.90. Here's the catch: You still can't make a profit because of that $10 commission. You can either keep on holding the stock for a few more years, or you can sell it and try to buy something more profitable (although if you're making 10% per year on any investment, you're doing pretty well!).

Let's say the company has a bad year and the stock loses 20% of its value. Yow! That stinks! Now it's worth only $72. What should you do?

- YOUR STOCK -
$ELL

SELL
You decide to sell the stock. With the commission fee, you end up with only $62 to your name. You lost more than 30% of your money, but now you can try to invest it in something more profitable. Best of luck to you!

HOLD
You hang tight, hoping that the stock will rise to its former value. In fact, you hold on to it for 20 years. It has its ups and downs, but over time it does regain its value and then some.

FACEBOOK— LIKE OR UNLIKE?

Facebook held its initial public offering (aka an **IPO**, which is when a private company "goes public" and starts selling shares on the stock market) on May 18, 2012. The IPO was one of the biggest in technology, and the biggest in Internet history. Facebook was offered at $38.00/share on the first day of trading, but in the coming months the stock price would eventually fall as low as $17.55/share. However, by the end of 2015 the stock price was back up, hovering around $100/share. If you "liked" Facebook at the right time, you would have bought in when everyone "unliked" the stock, and would be well on your way to making $1 million! Why don't you check the price of Facebook stock today? Do it on your phone. G'head, we'll wait. Is it still climbing?

TAKE A BREATH

IT'S important to keep a close watch on your investments—but not *too* close. Some people love tracking their investments daily. Others get freaked-out at the slightest drop and make silly decisions. Depending on how long you're planning to invest, you could review them daily, weekly, monthly, or even every three months for a retirement account you won't be tapping for 50 years (assuming you don't make $1 million and retire by age 15). Keep an eye on the news and markets in general to spot risks and opportunities, and enjoy knowing you've done the right thing and invested the money for your future.

CAPITAL GAINS

CAPITAL gains taxes are taxes paid on profits from selling stocks. If you buy and then sell a stock less than a year later, the gains are taxed higher than if you hold the stock for more than a year. Before you sell your stock, find out the tax implications. You might talk to a broker or an accountant about this because taxes can vary by state. For kids who don't earn much income during the year, it may not make much of an impact.

THE CLOSING BELL

THERE is way more to investing than what we're able to say in this chapter. *Way* more! But hopefully we've inspired you to take the first few steps because investing can be one of the best ways to reach your goal of making $1 million.

The big lesson here? It's your money, it's your investment, and it's your responsibility. Taking the time to do your research, not getting in over your head, and making rational decisions are all critical to success. The best part is you're still young and have time to make up for any mistakes. So get investing because time is on your side!

LONG STORY SHORT

1. *All investments come with risk.*

2. *Do your research.*

3. *ONLY INVEST MONEY YOU CAN AFFORD TO LOSE.*

4. *Diversify to spread the risk.*

Chapter 10:
HOW NOT TO BECOME A MILLIONAIRE

BY this time you might be thinking: *What a great book! It's stuffed full of ways to become rich! All I have to do is follow this advice and I'll have so much cash, I can use it to line my parrot's cage. What could go wrong?*

Well, lots. There are many ways to achieve your financial goals—but there are many more ways to end up with nothing.

Here are the most common ways to blow your dough and keep yourself out of the million-dollar club.

1. EARN LESS THAN YOU SPEND.

It seems pretty obvious, but this is the number one reason people don't build up substantial wealth—even people who make a lot of money. A surgeon who carves out $50,000 a month but spends $60,000 will end up worse off than a custodial technician who sweeps up $2,000 a month and socks one-third of it away in the bank.

The cure: Make a budget (reread chapter 3 if you need a refresher). No matter how much money you make, if you don't keep track of what you're spending, you're going to blow it.

2. LOAD UP ON DEBT.

Although good for an emergency or an occasional big purchase, credit cards can gobble up your money. If you rely on a credit card, you could end up paying a big interest charge every month if you don't pay off the balance, and that money goes directly in the bank's pocket instead of yours.

The cure: Whenever possible, pay cash or use a debit card for your purchases. If you don't have the cash, save up until you have enough to afford it.

3. NO PLAN.

People without a financial plan don't know where they are going financially. And without goals it's easy to lose sight of the long-term objective and spend your hard-earned money on something silly.

The cure: Make a plan with short–, medium–, and long–term financial goals. Revisit your plan often to make sure it's lining up with your current goals.

4. GAMBLE.

For the vast majority of people, gambling means losing. Otherwise, casinos would all go out of business and states would not make any money off the lottery. Just remember this simple phrase: "The

house always wins in the end."

The cure: Don't do it. You'll rarely find a successful millionaire who won their money through gambling. And the vast majority of people who do win the lottery or a gambling jackpot end up blowing it all. There are no short-cuts to a million dollars.

5. FALL FOR CONS, SCAMS, FRAUDS, AND FLIM-FLAMS. Call them what

you will, the sad truth is people have thought up a lot of ways to rip you off.

The cure: Know your scams—and avoid them. Here are some common ways people will try to separate you from your money.

- Pyramid scheme: A "business" model where one person makes money by selling memberships in the business. People who get in early get paid, while others make little or nothing.

- Ponzi scheme: Similar to a pyramid scheme, a **Ponzi scheme** gets you to "invest" but pays you with the money others "invested," rather than with money earned by the idea. Only the scammer makes any real money.

- Phishing: You might get an email from a company asking you to confirm your account information, your credit card number, or your debit card PIN, or to pay some fee. This is likely a scammer trying to get at your money. *No* real company will ask for that kind of information by email.

- Identity theft: This occurs when people steal your personal info so they can pretend to be you and spend your money. How do they do it? Just a few critical bits of information like your

Loading up on credit card debt will only make your dreams of saving millions evaporate.

birthday, passwords, or Social Security number can be enough for people to gain access to your accounts. Protect the PIN number on your debit cards, tear up any mail with personal info, don't let mail linger in the mailbox, and safeguard all your personal info.

• Scholarship scams: These scams ask for money up front to apply, or tell you they know of "secret" scholarships, or try to get a credit card number. Scholarship information is free and publicly available, and real scholarships never require you to pay.

WHEN BAD THINGS HAPPEN TO SMART PEOPLE

WHAT about the stuff that's out of your hands? Financial misfortune can happen to even the most prepared people. Maybe you get an illness that's not covered by your health insurance. Life can be pretty harsh.

What do you do? Expect that bad stuff might happen and prepare for it.

That's why experts recommend setting some money aside in a separate "emergency fund" (at least three to six months' worth of income).

Insurance is another way to protect yourself financially—especially auto, medical, and life insurance. General liability insurance will protect you if you own a business.

DOWN BUT NOT OUT

SURE, if you want to make a million dollars, it helps if you don't lose the money you have. But even if things do go badly and you find yourself back close to zero, *do not* think that it's all over.

Here are just a couple of famous

Remember to watch out for those pesky badgers.

folks who bounced back from financial misfortune:

Walt Disney lost his first film-making company when a crooked distributor left him with no money. He lived off canned beans for five years before he scratched together every penny he had for a one-way bus ticket to California. There he created a cartoon mouse you've probably heard of. Things went better for him after that.

J. K. Rowling, the author of *Harry Potter*, was living in relative poverty before she wrote the bestselling book series. It became the biggest money-making series in history, making her billions. Today she is one of the richest women in the United Kingdom.

Each had periods of their lives when things were pretty bleak. But they kept at it and were able to reverse their fortunes. If financial misfortune happens to you, pull yourself back up and get back in the game because that million bucks ain't gonna walk into your pocket all by itself.

LONG STORY SHORT

1. *Don't spend more than you make.*

2. *Don't load up on debt.*

3. *Don't forget to make a plan with goals.*

4. *Don't gamble.*

5. *Don't fall for a scam.*

Conclusion:
GET GOING!

WELL, that's our book. We hope you use it as a springboard for ideas on how to make a million dollars. The fact that you're starting early gives you a *huge* advantage.

Just remember to use your newly acquired Million-Dollar Mind-Set so

you don't have to actually save up one million individual $1 bills, just enough so that it compounds into $1 million. How much is that? Depends on how soon you start saving, how much you save, how much compounding interest your investments earn over

WHERE DO MILLIONAIRES GET THEIR MONEY?

According to Brian Tracy, an entrepreneur, author, and professional development trainer, 99% of self-made millionaires come from these four categories:

- 74% started their own business.

- 10% are folks who climbed the corporate ladder into a senior executive position.

- 10% are professionals who get paid a lot, such as doctors, lawyers, accountants, and so on.

- 5% are salespeople and sales consultants who are really good at selling stuff.

your lifetime, and how disciplined you can be. We know people who've reached that goal within 10 years. Others are still on their way. Either way, *time is money*. Usually, the longer you let your savings and investments grow, the bigger they get. Keep track of your investments without obsessing over them, and occasionally adjust your plan, goals, budget, and investments to get a little bit better rate of return over the years. If you can keep adding money in baby steps, you'll soon see your savings climbing past the $100,000 mark, then $250,000, $500,000 $800,000, $999,999.99. Don't forget to celebrate when you reach $1,000,000—you've earned it!

IT'S NEVER TOO LATE

NOT everyone can start saving early, but there are lots of ways to make it to $1 million.

Let's say you are not able to start saving until you're 30 years old, but then you put away $250 per month for the next 15 years. By the time you're 45, at 7% interest, you'll have $80,664.16 saved up. After that if you can bump up savings to $300 a month, then you'll make it to $1 million by the time you're 75. But you'll need to get slightly better than 7% return on your investments to achieve your goal. You'll need to be a lot more aggressive with your investments. Moral of this story? *Start now!*

TALK TO A PRO

Part of being smart about money is knowing when to call in the experts.

THERE are lots of ways to reach your ultimate goal: Finding the right balance among earning, saving, and investing is something you'll have to figure out for yourself. That doesn't mean going it alone. A lot of people will work with a financial adviser or an accountant to help them manage their money. Many schools have financial literacy classes, and you can join an investment club. There are a lot of people and companies that offer free help. And if you check online, the amount of information is stunning.

Still, some of the best (or worst—be careful!) advice can come from family. Some families don't like to talk about money and finance with kids. Others don't find it a problem. We think that talking about money is a good thing because it helps teach everybody about the family's finances. Maybe you can throw the folks a tip or two about compounding their savings or turn them on to a stock that splits four times every two years.

KEEP LEARNING

THERE is so much more cool stuff to discover when it comes to the world of money and finance. The more you learn, the better chance you have at succeeding financially. With a plan, goals, focus, patience, time, resilience, perseverance, quick thinking, and a little luck, you should be able to make it to at least a million dollars. Don't sell yourself short.

WE'RE NOT TALKING ABOUT GREED

WE need you to stop thinking like a kid for a moment and imagine what your life will be like when you're wrinkled like a prune.

Retirement. Ahhh, the good life: golfing, argyle socks, denture cream, unlimited naps. Unfortunately, a good chunk of Americans are going to spend their "retirement" working—given that 36% of them don't save anything for it. About that same number rely totally on **Social Security** (a government fund that working people are required to pay into, which then provides money to them after they reach a certain age of retirement). Whether or not it's possible to live on Social Security alone, it's not exactly the most fun way to spend your golden years! In fact, the average savings of a 50-year-old American is just $43,797. That won't last very long. And with people living longer (sometimes 30 or more years between the time you retire and the time you expire), that means you'll need a lot more cash to pay for your robotic joints. So don't be a chump with no money left for golf balls. Get into a Million-Dollar Mind-Set and start putting away money now.

YOU MADE A MILLION DOLLARS? GREAT. NOW, ZIP IT

FLASHING your cash, driving a fancy car, wearing designer shoes, playing the high roller to impress people . . . all that can make you look like a fool. It can also invite theft. Many millionaires have had their money or possessions stolen. Why invite the risk? If you are thinking like a millionaire, you'll know to keep a low profile and just be quietly awesome.

The sooner—and harder—you work, the sooner you can enjoy the rewards.

SAVE, SPEND, AND ESPECIALLY SHARE: MILLIONAIRES WHO SPREAD THE WEALTH

Many millionaires make donations to charities and causes they really care about. Giving money to help others is one of the best feelings in the world. Ask any millionaire philanthropist.

BILL GATES

When it comes to a multimillionaire (okay, billionaire) giving to charity, one person comes to mind. As the founder of Microsoft, Bill Gates is often cited as one of the wealthiest men on the planet. Bill and his wife, Melinda, started the Bill & Melinda Gates Foundation, which has an endowment of about $33.5 billion, and addresses world health issues. Bill Gates also took the "Giving Pledge," where he has sought out wealthy people to commit to give away a majority of their wealth to good causes.

MARK ZUCKERBERG

At 23, the Facebook CEO became one of the world's youngest billionaires and had already started making large contributions to charities. They include $100 million to help fix the public school system in New Jersey and $120 million for schools in the Bay Area, which is part of a larger donation of more than $1 billion worth of Facebook stock to the Silicon Valley Community Foundation.

OPRAH WINFREY

Oprah has donated millions of dollars to various charities and organizations, with most of her money going to her own three foundations. She also supports a leadership academy for girls in South Africa (which she started), efforts to rebuild the Gulf Coast, a charity that rescues abandoned babies, and a charity that builds schools in third-world countries. Once she even gave everyone in the audience of her daytime talk show $1,000 each for the charity of their choice. Now that's philanthropy!

ONE MILLION DOLLARS!

IT is possible to be poor and happy, or rich and sad, but people who are financially independent have a lot less to worry about than people who are crushed by debt or struggling to pay the bills each month.

Although this book is all about making enough to live a comfortable existence, we hope you realize it's also about enjoying the journey and having fun while you learn to make your million. We also hope you share what you've learned. Maybe by becoming financially independent you're better able to support your community, help lift others out of poverty, and get more kids on the path to financial security. Maybe you'll be so successful, you'll write your own book on how to earn, save, and invest your way to $10 million! And just think, it all started with a goal of saving $100.

Whatever your future, we hope you find financial success and happiness. So get out there and give it your best shot. We'll be here cheering you on while you turn $100 into $1 million.

Good luck!

LONG STORY SHORT

We already made a long story short by writing this book, so if you didn't read it, there's nothing we can do to help you now.

YOUR PATH TO $1 MILLION CHECKLIST

Go ahead. Take that first step, no matter how small it is, to reach your goal of making a million dollars. Check each box below along the way and track your journey on the next page.

☐ Develop a Million-Dollar Mind-Set.

☐ Open a savings account at a bank or credit union.

☐ Set financial goals and develop a budget—and stick to them.

☐ Increase your earning power by getting a job or starting a business.

☐ Save up $100, then make regular saving a habit.

☐ Got a few hundred bucks? Move some of your money from your savings account into other investments to maximize interest.

☐ Move some money into an emergency fund. It should equal at least three to six months of your income.

☐ Use the power of time and compound interest to really grow, grow, grow your bucks.

☐ Avoid all the dumb things people do to lose money once they have it.

☐ Go play golf (or Ultimate Frisbee) like a millionaire.

YOUR TWO-PAGE PLAN TO BECOME A MILLIONAIRE

NAME: _____

AGE: _____

GOAL: _____ $1,000,000! _____

_____

_____

COMMITMENT STATEMENT

Add your current age to the number of years you think it will take to become a millionaire. Look at yourself in the mirror and repeat this statement:

"I, _____,
WILL BECOME A MILLIONAIRE BY THE TIME
I AM _____ YEARS OLD."

(Be realistic. Give yourself enough time and modify as you go along.)

SETTING FINANCIAL GOALS

List your short-, medium-, and long-term goals. (Your long-term goal should be $1,000,000 or more.)

Short-term goal (under 1 year):

$_____

Medium-term goal (1 to 10 years):

$_____

Long-term goal (10+ years):

$_____

EARNING INCOME

List all the ways you'll get money to achieve your goals:

Allowance: _____

_____

Work/Job: _____

_____

Extra Jobs: _____

_____

Start a Business: _____

_____

Interest on Investments: _____

_____

Gifts/Inheritance: _____

KEEPING A BUDGET

Create a budget that will help you achieve your financial goals (and don't forget to set up a savings account!):

MONTHLY INCOME: $_____
MONTHLY EXPENSES: $_____
Savings (Pay Yourself First): $_____
Transportation: $_____
Phone bill: $_____
Media downloads: $_____
School supplies: $_____
Food: $_____
Clothes: $_____
Entertainment: $_____
Other: $_____
Total: $_____

If your expenses total more than income, you'll blow your budget. Revise!

CHECKING IN AND REVISING

Check your progress with your goals—do it yearly, monthly, or weekly. How are you doing? Do you need to revise anything?:

_____

Who can help you with this? Be your mentor? Hold you accountable?:

_____

How often will you check in with them?: _____

YOUR ONE-PAGE BUSINESS PLAN

BUSINESS NAME

THE "BIG IDEA"

MARKETING MADNESS

PRODUCT: What are you selling and who will buy it? _____

PRICE: How much will you charge for your product or service? _____

PLACE: Where can people buy your product or service? _____

PROMOTION: How will you get the word out? _____

MAKE A PROFIT

Calculate your profit potential for a one-month period.

TOTAL INCOME: _____
TOTAL EXPENSES: _____
PROFIT = (INCOME MINUS EXPENSES): _____

Making a profit? Great! You're off to a good start. If not, go back and see if you can increase your income or decrease your expenses. What's next? Make sure you hand out your plan to family, friends, and potential investors!

DRAW YOUR BUSINESS LOGO

YOUR PERSONAL BUDGET TRACKER

Here's a simple budget tracker to help you get started. Photocopy it five times, and you've got yourself a one-month budget to play with. Each day enter any income earned and expenses owed.

---MONDAY---

INCOME

Item   Amount

_____|_____
_____|_____
_____|_____

Total: _____

EXPENSES

Item   Amount

_____|_____
_____|_____
_____|_____
_____|_____
_____|_____

Total: _____

---TUESDAY---

INCOME

Item   Amount

_____|_____
_____|_____
_____|_____

Total: _____

EXPENSES

Item   Amount

_____|_____
_____|_____
_____|_____
_____|_____
_____|_____

Total: _____

--WEDNESDAY--

INCOME

Item   Amount

_____|_____
_____|_____
_____|_____

Total: _____

EXPENSES

Item   Amount

_____|_____
_____|_____
_____|_____
_____|_____
_____|_____

Total: _____

---THURSDAY---

INCOME

Item   Amount

_____|_____
_____|_____
_____|_____

Total: _____

EXPENSES

Item   Amount

_____|_____
_____|_____
_____|_____
_____|_____
_____|_____

Total: _____

---FRIDAY---

INCOME

Item   Amount

_____|_____
_____|_____
_____|_____

Total: _____

EXPENSES

Item   Amount

_____|_____
_____|_____
_____|_____
_____|_____

Total: _____

---SATURDAY---

INCOME

Item   Amount

_____|_____
_____|_____
_____|_____

Total: _____

EXPENSES

Item   Amount

_____|_____
_____|_____
_____|_____
_____|_____

Total: _____

---SUNDAY---

INCOME

Item   Amount

_____|_____
_____|_____
_____|_____

Total: _____

EXPENSES

Item   Amount

_____|_____
_____|_____
_____|_____
_____|_____

Total: _____

Glossary

ACCOUNT STATEMENT a written report of your finances.

BANK a business that keeps money for individual people or companies, exchanges currencies, makes loans, and offers other financial services.

BE PERSISTENT you know what that means, but it's important enough to say it again—be persistent!

BOND a debt instrument issued by a government or company promising to pay back borrowed money at a fixed rate of interest on a specified date.

BORROWER a person who gets money for a period of time knowing that the money must be returned.

BROKER a specially licensed person who trades stocks on the exchanges for other people.

BROKERAGE ACCOUNT like a bank account, but with a brokerage firm.

BUDGET a plan specifying how resources, especially time or money, will be allocated or spent during a particular period.

BULL OR BEAR MARKET a bull market is a period of generally rising prices. A bear market is a general decline in the stock market over a period of time.

BUSINESS PLAN a plan that sets out the future strategy and financial development of a business, usually covering a period of several years.

BUY LOW AND SELL HIGH when buying and selling stock in particular, it's best to purchase when the cost is low and then sell when the price is high, thus increasing your profit (much easier said than done).

CAREER a job or occupation regarded as a long-term or lifelong activity.

CD (CERTIFICATE OF DEPOSIT) similar to a savings account in that it is insured and thus virtually risk-free, though it requires a deposit for a set period of time.

COMMISSION a fee paid to an agent for providing a service, especially a percentage of the total amount of business transacted.

COMPOUND INTEREST interest calculated on the initial principal and also on the accumulated interest of previous periods of a deposit or loan.

CREDIT a loan of money between a borrower and a lender. The debt is then repaid through a series of payments, plus interest. A credit card is a classic example.

CREDIT UNION a cooperative savings association that offers financial services to its members at reduced interest rates.

CROWD FUNDING the practice of raising funds from a large group of people (usually) over the Internet toward a common service, project, product, investment, cause, or experience.

CUSTODIAL ACCOUNT an account managed by somebody other than the person who benefits from it, e.g., by a parent for a child.

DEBT an amount of money, a service, or an item of property that is owed to somebody.

DIRECT DEPOSIT a paycheck electronically deposited into your bank account.

DIVERSIFICATION reducing your risk by having a variety of investments. We can't explain it any better than "don't put all your eggs in one basket."

DIVIDEND stockholders' share of a company's profit, paid either in cash or more shares.

ECONOMIC DOWNTURN a drop or reduction in the success of a business or economy.

EMERGENCY FUND money saved for unexpected expenses, such as having to replace the phone you dropped in the toilet.

EXCHANGE where the trading of commodities, securities, or other assets takes place.

EXPENSES the amount of money spent in order to buy or do something.

FINANCIAL FREEDOM having enough money to live comfortably without actively working, if you don't want to. What that amount may be is up to you. For some, it is more than a million dollars. For others, it is less than a million dollars.

FRAUD the crime of obtaining money or some other benefit by deliberate deception.

GREAT DEPRESSION OF THE 1930s the deepest and longest economic downturn in U.S. history, which started with the Stock Market Crash of October 1929.

GREAT RECESSION OF 2008 an economic downturn that began in December 2007, when 8.4 million people lost their jobs in the U.S.

INCOME the amount of money received over a period of time as payment for work, goods, services, or investments.

INDEX the average price of a chosen group of stocks traded on an exchange like the NYSE or NASDAQ.

INDEX FUND a mutual fund that invests in companies listed in an important stock market index in order to match the market's overall performance.

INHERITANCE something, often money or goods, passed on when a person dies.

INTEREST a small fee that a borrower pays to a lender.

INTERNSHIP a method of on-the-job training.

INVESTING putting money into a business, project, property, and so on, with the plan of making more money.

IPO (INITIAL PUBLIC OFFERING) when shares of stock in a company are sold to the general public, on a securities exchange, for the first time.

IRA short for an Individual Retirement Arrangement, it's an untaxed retirement account that often contains investments like stocks, bonds, certificates of deposit, and more. You just can't withdraw the money until you've reached a certain age.

IRS (INTERNAL REVENUE SERVICE) a government agency in charge of collecting taxes; you don't want to mess with them.

JOB INTERVIEW a meeting during which a job applicant is asked questions; it is a way for an employer to get to know you better.

LENDER a person or institution that offers money with the understanding it will be returned.

LISTED describes a company that has been listed on a stock market exchange (like in a grocery store) so people can buy/sell shares in it.

LOAN when one person borrows money from another. This debt is repaid by the borrower to the lender, usually with interest.

LONG-TERM GOAL a plan ranging over at least 10 years.

MARKET CAPITALIZATION the stock price of a publicly traded company multiplied by all the shares owned.

MARKETING the process of communicating the value of a product or service to customers.

MEDIUM-TERM GOAL a plan of action completed in fewer than 10 years.

MOGUL No, not a mound of hard compacted snow, but a powerful person in a certain industry.

MUTUAL FUND a collection of investments, purchased by money collected from many investors. Mutual funds are generally not insured like a savings account. They are an investment tool, usually managed by a Fund Manager, so check for fees and know the success history of the fund before you invest.

PAY YOURSELF FIRST (PYF) just like it sounds—put money into your savings before you start paying bills, spending it, or giving it away.

P/E RATIO the relationship between the stock price and the company's earnings (profit) per share of stock.

PONZI SCHEME a pyramid investment swindle, named after Charles Ponzi

(1882–1949), in which supposed "profits" are paid to early investors from money actually invested by later participants. Ponzi was a businessman and con artist who became known in the early 1920s as a swindler for his moneymaking scheme.

PORTFOLIO the group of stocks, bonds, real estate, or anything else you have invested your money in.

PRINCIPAL here we mean the money you start with, not the person whom you get sent to when you act out in class.

PRODUCT the material sold as finished goods, also known as a commodity.

PROFIT what's left over when you subtract expenses from revenues.

PROFIT POTENTIAL how much money can you really make (a little more specific than "the sky's the limit").

PROSPECTUS a legal document that has all the information about a business that someone might want to invest in.

PRIVATE VERSUS PUBLIC COMPANY a privately owned company is owned by private investors, shareholders, or owners; there is no way you can invest in one. Whereas a publicly owned company offers its securities (stock/shares, bonds/loans, etc.) for sale.

RATE OF RETURN a profit on an investment over a period of time, expressed as a percentage of the original investment.

RATING AGENCY a company that issues credit ratings for the debt of public and private corporations.

RECORD a music disc made of vinyl that would sometimes break and play the same thing over and over and over and over and over and over.

REFERENCE a statement concerning somebody's (your) character or qualifications from someone you know or have worked for.

RÉSUMÉ a written description of your work experience and education, usually on one page.

RETIREMENT when you've done everything in this book, made your million dollars, and no longer need to work for a living.

RISK AND REWARD offsetting the chance of something going bad (risk) with the hope something will be very good (reward).

RULE OF 72 a simple method for roughly determining how long it will take for an investment to double in value at a specific rate of interest.

SAVINGS ACCOUNT a bank account that earns interest on money deposited.

SERVICE a set of actions performed to benefit your customers.

SHARE a way of measuring ownership of something. For example, you might own a "share" of a company by purchasing it on the stock market. You can own one share, or millions of shares, in one investment, or many.

SHORT-TERM GOAL an immediate plan of action.

SIMPLE INTEREST a quick way to calculate the cost of interest only on the principal of a loan.

SOCIAL SECURITY a social insurance program run by the federal government that gives out retirement, disability, and survivors' benefits.

STATE LABOR LAWS rules in each state that protect the rights and state the duties of workers and employers.

STOCK a share in the capital of a company or a unit of ownership (specifically, "common stock").

STOCK MARKET A market where securities are bought and sold.

STOCK SPLIT the division of shares of stock so that shareholders receive more shares at a proportionately lower value, leaving the total value unchanged.

TAKE A LOSS when you sell off your investment and lose money (boo).

TAKE A PROFIT when you sell off your investment and make money (yay).

TARGET MARKET the specific customers that a company wants to sell its products or services to.

UNDERVALUE to judge the value (worth) of a company as being lower than it really is (or how you may feel after you've done all your chores and no one says thank-you).

VALUE INVESTING investment in stocks believed to be worth far more than their current prices.

WALL STREET a street in New York City that runs through the historical center of the Financial District, which contains the headquarters of many of the city's major financial institutions. It's also the home of the world's largest stock exchange, the New York Stock Exchange, and a figure of speech for all the financial markets of the United States as a whole.

WANT something that would be nice to have but you can literally live without.

WINDFALL a significant, unexpected, large amount of money received at one time.

ABOUT THE AUTHORS

James McKenna and Jeannine Glista, along with Erren Gottlieb and Jamie Hammond, are co-creators of Biz Kid$, a national financial education initiative based on the Emmy Award–winning, nationally syndicated public TV series of the same name. James, Erren, and Jamie all live and save their money in Seattle, WA. Jeannine lives and saves her money in Nevada City, CA.

Matt Fontaine is a writer who lives, and saves his money, on Vashon Island, WA. You can find him at thinksmartmouth.com.

The *Biz Kid$* series has been seen by more than 15 million people worldwide since its premiere in 2008. It is broadcast worldwide and accessible through numerous outlets. The series is co-created and co–executive-produced by the creators of *Bill Nye the Science Guy*. It has also been approved as a financial education recommended resource in 16 states. Biz Kid$ is complemented by a resource-rich website with free lesson plans, online games, and community activities at bizkids.com.